THE DISCUS IN THE COMMUNITY TANK

Bernd Degen

Bernd Degen

THE DISCUS
in the community tank

CONTENTS

®
1993 Tetra-Press
Tetra-Werke
Dr. rer nat. Ulrich Baensch GmbH
P. O. Box 15 80 · D-49304 Melle,
Germany

1st etition 1 — 6.200, 1993
Translation: Mick Parry, Leadbury, U.K.
Typesetting: Fotosatz Hoffmann, Hennef
Printed in Germany
Distributed in U.S.A. by
TetraSales (Division of Warner Lambert)
3001 Commerce Street
Blacksburg, Virginia 24060 — 6671
WL-Code: 16585

ISBN 1-56465-121-5

FOREWORD

The discus is the real king of the freshwater
aquarium even though it may lag behind
the neon tetra in the league table of
ornamental fish sales. If a king is defined as
someone who stands out from the crowd,
then the discus can be classed as truly regal.
He quickly gets to know his keeper and
displays enormous curiosity as he patrols
the aquarium at feeding time. Generally
they make fascinating aquarium subjects
and breeding them is a stimulating and
rewarding pastime.

They have gained an unjustified reputa-
tion for being rather sensitive, susceptible
fish whereas, in fact, the opposite is true.
What other fish is as forgiving of the many
sins that are perpetrated by their keepers?

This book is intended as a contribution
to making the discus known amongst a
wider circle of hobbyists and to encoura-
ging more of them to take up keeping these
delightful fish. My purpose is specifically
to promote the cause of the discus for
those potential discus fans who are con-
sidering introducing them into their home
aquarium. For those who have already been
converted and who may want to progress
to breeding and raising this fish, there is
already a vast range of specialist literature
available. I hope to succeed in rousing the
curiosity of as many hobbyists as possible
so as to win over as many new fans of this
magnificent fish as it rightfully deserves.

Bernd Degen

THE AMAZONIAN WORLD

If we take a look at the Amazonas river basin on a map of South America, we will soon appreciate why it is classed as the longest and biggest river system on earth. In its entirety this basin, consisting in all of over one thousand individual rivers, drains seven million square kilometres of land.

With its overall length of 6516 km, the River Amazonas acts as the focal point for all the tributaries. This gigantic river is by far the biggest body of fresh water on earth. Around 200,000 cubic metres of water per second discharge into the ocean at its vast mouth between Belem and Macapá.

This river basin which, if transposed to Europe, would stretch from the westernmost point of Portugal to Moscow, contains three distinct types of water. The various rivers are categorised into white water, black water or clear water rivers, according to their water colour. The rivers that carry the loamy-yellow, cloudy, white water such as the Rio Amazonas, Rio Solimoes,

Enclosed "lagos" — lakes left when the high water recedes — afford professional catchers the best prospects.

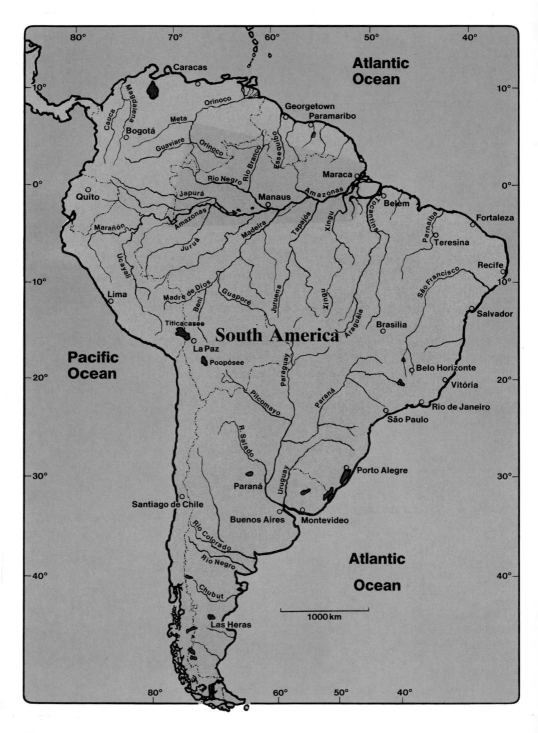

Rio Madeira, Rio Purus, Rio Jurua and the Rio Ucayali rise in the western part of South America, more specifically, from the Andes. The larger clear water rivers with their yellowy-green, transparent water — like the Rio Araguaia, Rio Xingu and the Rio Tapajos — rise in the south and flow north into Amazonas. The Rio Branco is the only clear water river that rises in the north of the continent to join the blackish-brown current of the Rio Negro.

The Rio Negro, one of Brazil's most important rivers, belongs to the black water group, as its name implies. The waters of these rivers are a transparent coffee brown colour and all flow down from the north into the white water rivers. The varying proportions that make up the

Piranhas make excellent eating although they have gained worldwide notoriety for their own voracious appetite.

resultant mixtures offer ideal living conditions for fish.

The white water rivers carry down countless tons of sediments and floating material from the highlands. These substances may be carried by the river systems all the way from the high Andes down to the Atlantic coast. The high concentration of a wide range of minerals is reflected in the relatively high pH of the white water. Whereas the black water rivers like the Rio Negro have an average pH value of around 4.5, the white water rivers are generally about the 6.5 mark.

The huge quantities of sediment are deposited on the floor of the flooded jungle during the high water period. It is about the start of the year when the waters start to rise. At this point the riverine forest along the banks becomes inundated and lake-like stretches of water, so-called Varzea lakes, form on the hinterland. In these flooded zones the water quickly loses its strong current and, as the waters become calm, they deposit the materials they are

The clear water rivers of Amazonas carry surprisingly clean, transparent water with very little sediment.

A mass of **Rio Negro** water looks like it came straight from the teapot. A tumblerful of it though does not show any sign of this brownish tint.

Fixed keep nets like this one are used to hold any captured fish prior to shipment on to wholesalers in Manaus. There may be a delay of some weeks but at least the fish have a better chance of survival than in plastic containers.

carrying. These tremendous amounts of sediment mean that the banks and contours of the river are subject to constant changes. Sandbanks in the rivers alter their position dramatically as well, representing a constant challenge to the pilots of boats.

This means that regular disembarkation to shove a boat free from such an underwater hazard is more or less the order of the day during any boat trip on the Amazonas.

If the water level falls rapidly — as it can during the dry period — boats with a fairly deep draught may be left stranded high and dry and can only be refloated when the waters rise in the next wet season.

One of the favourite labels that travellers to Amazonas are wont to use when describing the tropical rain forest is "Green Hell" and indeed the prospect of trying to go it alone in this jungle is somewhat daunting. But the seemingly endless expanse of rivers and forests exerts an incomparable attraction on its admirers so that a stay in Amazonas can turn into a true holiday experience.

It is by no means true to state that your every step could be dogged by the threat of piranhas, venomous snakes or bloodthirsty crocodiles. The locals bathe and swim in their stretch of river as if it were the most natural thing in the world. During daylight hours and provided you show a healthy amount of care in respect of the vagaries of the currents, there is practically no risk at all. Accidents involving piranhas, those notorious predatory fish with the razor-sharp teeth, only really occur when people fish for them. Once caught, the piranhas, naturally enough, tend to scythe around with their teeth snapping at everything within reach.

The local species of crocodile, known as the jacaré, does not grow to anything like the length seen in films portraying Tarzan's latest adventure, especially as they have been ruthlessly hunted to the verge of extinction. At night the crocodiles often lie on the river banks and if a flashlight is shone in their eyes, these will light up like burning coals.

The rain forest is home to a multitude of plants and animals though a hike through it will fairly soon reveal that there is little of

Typical boats used for fish catching in Barcelos, a little shanty town north of Manaus on the Rio Negro.

interest for the naturalist on the actual forest floor itself.

The thick undergrowth is by no means easy to penetrate. Scarcely any animals are to be seen and there is no trace of any of the glamorous orchids often associated with these parts. The explanation lies in the fact that so little light can get through the plant canopy to reach the forest floor. This means that the plants have to migrate ever upwards in order to find conditions where they can thrive. It is in the tops of the trees that one finds the orchids, bromeliads and other parasitic plants! The colourful birds also fly over the tops of the trees and are often best seen from the boats.

The author examines a HECKEL-discus caught on the Rio Negro where large numbers of this species occur. Magnificent specimens can be obtained for the price of a packet of cigarettes.

A fish catcher's boat on the Amazon. The whole family lives here, sleeping in hammocks.

Any trip you make into the forest itself is bound to involve you in copious sweating because the high air humidity literally draws the sweat out of your pores. The unpleasant experience of the jungle is in stark contrast to the pleasant nature of living near to the river and for this reason you should only venture into the "bush" if accompanied by an experienced guide.

Added to this is the plague of mosquitoes and the associated risk of malaria which must not be underestimated. Generally speaking, if you make a trip along black water rivers like the Rio Negro, you will more or less be spared from the full horrors of mosquitoes but if you are following the course of the white water rivers, a protective net is essential. Presumably this phenomenon is in some way connected with the low pH value of black

water rivers which seem to be less productive.

The water quality also affects the varieties of fish that occur in the different rivers. To date no-one has managed to identify and chart the distribution of the various species of discus with any degree of accuracy. New localities are being found all the time. If one takes a good look at the map and considers the vast expanse of territory involved, then it seems logical that there must still be many of these rivers that have yet to have their fish populations fully charted.

Wild-caught discus are available through the trade at all times of the year and although there are some climatic constraints here, the aquarist can always obtain such specimens. The heavy rains begin in December in the Amazonas region and by

A typical **Amazonas** sky with some of the lovely cloud **formations** so often seen there. The vast expanses of this landscape often induce that "seaside holiday" feeling.

January and February the rivers rise to spectacular levels. For this reason the locals – often of mixed race known as "caboclos" – build their huts at least 15 metres above the normal low water mark. The floods then last well into June. During this rainy season discus are caught in the narrower side arms of the Amazonas. The main months for export are October to March. The fish are not exported at all during the months of May to August.

The beginnings of environmental awareness are now stirring in Brazil. This is reflected in the implementation of catch quotas for red neons. If one bears in mind that a local fisherman can expect to receive 100 cruzados – about one dollar – for an adult discus, then one can see just how valuable such a booty is for someone struggling to make a living. The survival of the discus is obviously of economic importance to the local fisherman.

Discus are often caught in fixed nets, a method which only requires one operator and so is favoured by the fisherman, who prefer to make their expeditions into the forest alone. Favourable areas are surrounded by nets, any driftwood is pulled out and then the nets are pulled together. The fish catch is then laboriously sorted.

The fishermen set out at night in a small boat into the side arms of the rivers, the lakes left by the floods or the quieter bank zones. Here the boat glides gently through the shallow water near the bank where the sleeping fish can easily be seen in waters up to one metre deep using the light from a flashlamp. They are effortlessly caught using only a hand net. The only troublesome fish are the nocturnal catfish that dart away from the approaching boats at a fast rate of knots occasionally disturbing the unsuspecting discus. This method of catching is ideally suited for discus, scalares and characins and very soon the plastic containers are filled with ornamental fish of all kinds. These are then transferred to the main boat for sorting into dozens of white plastic tanks that sit on the decks of the larger vessels. If the fisherman lives away from one of the main settlements, he will keep his catch in fixed nets in the river in front of his house. At the appropriate time he will then take his total catch to the large buyers and dealers in Manaus. Here the fish are kept for just a short while longer before they are sent on their great voyage half way across the world. It may be several weeks before a discus finally reaches its destination at a wholesaler.

ORIGIN OF THE DISCUS —
ITS SIGNIFICANCE FOR AQUARIUM LIFE

Discus fish originate from Amazonia, that is, from one of the great tropical regions of the world. This has certain logical implications for their general care in the aquarium.

To start with, their home waters have an average daytime temperature of 30 °C and this should be reflected in the home aquarium because discus love and will only thrive in warm water. However, as the majority of fishkeepers would like to keep their discus in planted aquaria, this need for warmth turns into something of a problem because aquatic plants in tanks do not generally tolerate such high tempera-tures. Most aquarium plants prefer mean temperatures of 25 °C. In this situation it is the wellbeing of the fish that should take precedence and a water temperature of 27 °C should be regarded as the absolute bottom limit. If at all possible, you should try to provide them with one or two degrees more. If kept in too cold condi-tions, discus will quickly show adverse effects. During the breeding season and in dedicated breeding and rearing tanks 29 to 30 °C should be regarded as standard. However, it is not just the temperature that is an important prerequisite if discus are to

One year old Red Turquoise Discus in a large well planted aquarium with some charming characins.

live happily in captivity. Water composition is a significant factor too. The hardness of their home waters is very low whilst the pH value is markedly in the acid range. Measurements carried out on the conductivity of the black water rivers of Amazonas produced values of around 10 Microsiemens (µS) which is almost infinitesimal. Nor are the figures very much higher in the white water rivers. For all that, taken as a whole, the water quality is stable in these rivers.

We cannot always offer our discus their very own "species-tailored" water from an original source, therefore we have to treat our tap water to produce something suitable. Our mains water comes out of the tap with properties that range wildly. For instance, in one town the general hardness may be 30° dH (German hardness) whilst in another it may only be 3° dH. Where the object is simply to keep a number of discus, a moderately hard water may be tolerated but for breeding purposes the keeper will need to intervene to reproduce the properties found in the Amazonas.

The third important factor for successful discus care is proper feeding. In this regard the discus in the wild leads a frugal existence. It could not be said that it is exactly spoilt by nature, especially in areas such as the black water regions that have a low insect population, such as the black water regions. Mosquito larvae are also not always accessible. Ephemera, or day flies, can occur in vast quantities in some places but it has not yet been proven whether these constitute a significant source of food

for discus. The tiny freshwater shrimps that occur in large numbers seem to be an acceptable item on the discus menu. However, as far as can be told from their feeding behaviour, it is only the smaller specimens that are taken.

So in captivity it is not a difficult task to whet the appetite of this species. Given their relatively catholic tastes and the wide range of speciality foods now offered by the trade, catering for discus in matters culinary is quite straightforward. One real step forward here is the recent introduction of a special discus food in dried form.

It is often said of wild-caught discus that they are very choosy when it comes to food. Long experience has shown, however, that even wild-caught specimens will accept any type of substitute food provided that the keeper gives some thought to how the diet is presented. By this I mean that the fish should be offered small portions of food at frequent, regular intervals. Any uneaten food should be removed quite quickly and the fish offered more soon after. This approach should meet with success after a couple of days of settling in. Once one fish decides it wants to start eating, the others will take up the habit, as much out of envy as anything, seemingly. A healthy discus will eat practically everything you can give it. With especially sensitive subjects, like the HECKEL discus, it can also be helpful to put an established, old stager into the same aquarium. The novice will soon be copying the master and develop a hearty appetite.

HISTORICAL DETAILS

The true king of the freshwater aquarium really ought to have some kind of royal ancestry. Indeed its breeding was surrounded by a web of secrecy for many, many years and the first successful attempts at breeding it in captivity were a long time coming.

Discus were first mentioned in the literature by the Vienna-based ichthyologist, DR. JOHANN JACOB HECKEL, in 1840. It was from him that the HECKEL discus group got its name. DR. HECKEL described a specimen he encountered in NATTERER's collection. It was at this point too that the Symphysodon discus were presented to the aquarium world for the first time. But it was many decades on that they were first bred in captivity.

Those specimens of Symphysodon discus had been discovered in the Rio Negro. This species is widely distributed in this river, particularly in the stretch just beyond where the Rio Branco discharges its massive volume of water into the main river. The mixture of black water and white water seems to be very much to the liking of these "HECKEL" discus.

In subsequent years scientists became more closely involved with the study of these fish but somehow no-one in Europe ever made a significant breakthrough. They achieved a certain notoriety as problematic breeders simply because nobody recognised the importance of the skin secretions for the larvae. This situation continued until 1959 when HARALD SCHULZ produced his in-depth report on the capture of discus fish. It was only around this time that any substantial numbers of wild-caught discus began arriving in Germany and were bred successfully in aquaria. By the same token, these fish could now be more widely available for hobbyists. To begin with discus changed hands at phenomenal prices. However, as time went by, more and more amateurs managed to breed these fish in their own aquaria and this was eventually reflected in their price. Even so, discus have still not become cheap and this is probably all to the good. For if they were a simple, unchallenging proposition, like

A splendid, wild-caught brown discus. One of its most noticeable features are the intense red borders to the fins. The dark hem on the fin is also typical of this colour variant.

the scalares, then they too would turn into a "mass production" fish and their regal aura would be lost.

So the discus fish has remained high on the list of interesting fish partly on the grounds of its high price. By virtue of this fact fishkeepers bestow on it the appropriate levels of care and attention. It is still not the easiest of subjects to breed and to achieve this is widely regarded as the pinnacle of achievement for people interested in the hobby.

Discus species in the wild

The original description of the discus genus gave it the name "Symphysodon" which then stood as the generic name. In 1840 HECKEL described the first species, Symphysodon discus, to which was added the name of the biologist responsible for the original description, resulting in the creation of the specific name Symphysodon discus HECKEL. Aquarist circles are wont to refer to this HECKEL discus as the "genuine article" in terms of discus, though this does not really represent any form of judgement on its aesthetic or qualitative standing.

Wild-caught specimens are something special in any species of fish. They still have something "wild" in their blood and it usually shows. They have not yet been subjected to the often deleterious intervention of man. Many discus fans would therefore be more than glad to have the chance to have a wild-caught specimen in their care. Even though the colours are perhaps not quite as startlingly brilliant as in many captive-bred specimens, they still have marvellous colouring. Anyone who has witnessed the impressive courtship display of fully grown discus in prime breeding condition

The Rio Negro's waters are the colour of black coffee and the banks are often of white sand. Local fishermen keep their catch in keep nets near the bank so that a constant supply of good water is at hand.

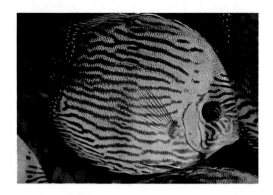

will be only too willing to overlook the stubborn fifth body stripe.

In any event they are to be thoroughly recommended.

Symphysodon discus HECKEL. Its basic coloration tends to drift from a violet grey through yellowy brown to a pale blue. Wavy longitudinal lines with a light blue, turquoise shimmer run the whole length of the body. This colour becomes dominant in the area of the head and fins. A typical characteristic of this species is the rather broad black transverse stripe that runs down through the middle of the body. A HECKEL discus can readily and easily be distinguished through this feature.

The colour of its eyes is usually amber or yellow with the conspicuous gleaming red eye rather uncommon in this species. It is mainly distributed in the Rio Negro. This species of discus is widely regarded as being the most difficult to keep. It is very fussy about its water quality and is very quick to react adversely to any deterioration in its environment. It is also more choosy about its food than its cogeners. Once it has settled in and begins to show

its true colours in a well planted aquarium, it is an absolute dream of a fish. Unfortunately, because of its pronounced vertical stripe, it leads something of a shadowy existence in the popularity scale amongst discus fans. For some reason or other, they are so put off by this feature that they show a good deal of reluctance to buy HECKEL discus. This is one of the reasons why it has failed to become well established as an aquarium fish. It is a fish for pure discus specialists.

In 1981 BURGESS described a subspecies of Symphysodon discus, named in honour of WILLI SCHWARTZ, the famous discus wholesaler who operated out of Manaus, and bearing the impressive title of Symphysodon discus willischwartzi. This subspecies is distinguished by its heavier greeny blue head stripes. The pronounced mid-stripe is present here too. In the trade these fish are referred to as blue-headed HECKELS. The basis for classifying this as a separate subspecies was its higher number of rows of scales, namely 53 to 59, as opposed to 45 to 53 in Symphysodon discus HECKEL.

Symphysodon aequifasciatus aequifasciatus PELLEGRIN was described in 1903 as the green discus by the Frenchman PELLEGRIN who was describing specimens that had been caught mainly in Lago Tefé. This had led to the green discus also being known under the popular nickname of "Tefé". Its basic colour is a greenish brown with nine transverse stripes, all equally defined. In the region of the pectoral and ventral fins, as well as near the head, greenish-blue stripes are clearly visible. The hem of the ventral fins is usually green coloured. It is also possible to find complete longi-

Symphysodon aequifasciatus axelrodi was described by SCHULTZ in 1960 as the brown discus. It is probably the best known of the wild-caught discus strains because it was with this fish that the first breeding successes were obtained. Its basic colouring is yellowy brown to dark brown. Its body is likewise crossed by nine dark transverse stripes, of which the first, above the eyes, is particularly well defined. The head, dorsal and ventral fins have just a few, though very beautiful, blue, longitudinal lines. On the pectoral fins and the other fin hems too, it is possible to make out a

tudinal striation of the body, showing greenish blue iridescent stripes. Such specimens are traded under the name of "Royal Green" discus, though this is strictly a trade name rather than a scientific one. Its eye colour may be yellow, amber or red.

Wild-caught green discus need a very long time before they take on their true full colouring. But with the lapse of time, what start out as quite inconspicuous sorts — "ugly ducklings" almost -later turn into glorious fish with quite stunning colours.

Now and again green discus turn up with beautiful red spots on their undersides. Such wild-caught specimens are highly sought after — with their desirability increasing with the number of their spots. In the trade they are known as "Tefé" discus, although they can also come from southern Colombia, notably the area around Letitia. In point of fact though, very few discus are exported out of Colombia.

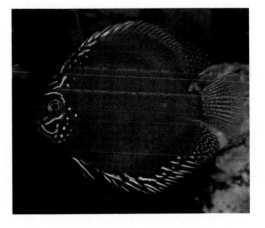

greater or lesser number of red markings. These fish are caught predominantly in the area around Belem. The eye colour here is usually red but yellow-eyed specimens are handled occasionally. This discus fish is amongst the least expensive and is often referred to as a "starter discus" for the beginner in this field. However, anyone

who has seen fully grown brown discus swimming around in a well planted aquarium will be the first to admit that it is just as interesting and beautiful as its flashy, brilliant turquoise counterparts. Because of the favourable price differential these brown discus are indeed well worth having as fish to learn the ropes of discus keeping. What is unquestionably beyond dispute is that the brown discus presents fewer problems in the aquarium than those results of highly selective breeding techniques, in their different shades of turquoise.

Another species is **Symphysodon aequifasciatus haraldi,** the blue discus, which was also described by SCHULTZ in 1960. The blue discus is found mainly in the area around Letitia and Benjamin Constant. The background colour of this species is also brownish. However, these fish have a more distinct, blue, longitudinal striping along the back, head and belly parts than is the case with the brown discus. Blue discus with complete blue striping are known as "Royal Blue" discus and are believed to be the most beautiful of wild-caught types, though unfortunately, top quality fish are rather rare. The eye is an intense red.

DISCUS SPECIES IN CAPTIVITY

As already stated, nature provides us with four different colour variants of discus, namely the brown, green and blue discus, as well as the HECKEL discus. Each of these colour variants has its own distinctive colour characteristics.

Once people succeeded in breeding wild-caught discus in captivity and in appreciable quantities, it was a natural progression for breeders to start wanting to use the finest specimens as stock for further selective breeding attempts. And, logically enough, this deliberate selection policy led in turn to improved colouring. In particular, the well-marked blue discus known as the "Royal Blue" was used to intensify the coloration of captive-bred hybrids. Similarly, many wild-caught specimens with a stronger green background colour were used to produce hybrids that were no longer dominated by a brownish basic hue. This proved to be the route to producing more and more discus that tended towards blue and turquoise. New tones were created. Through strict selection techniques lines of discus were developed that were given new trade names. Suddenly there were turquoise,

Turquoise discus, seen here in a well-designed and plant-filled aquarium, are the epitome of fish keeping.

brilliant, solid turquoise, cobalt-turquoise, red-turquoise discus and more besides. Almost every breeder was discovering amongst his batches of progeny identifiable colour strains which were duly given handy, "home-made" names. As a result it has become quite difficult to classify some of these "sports" correctly as there is no sound scientific basis for classification.

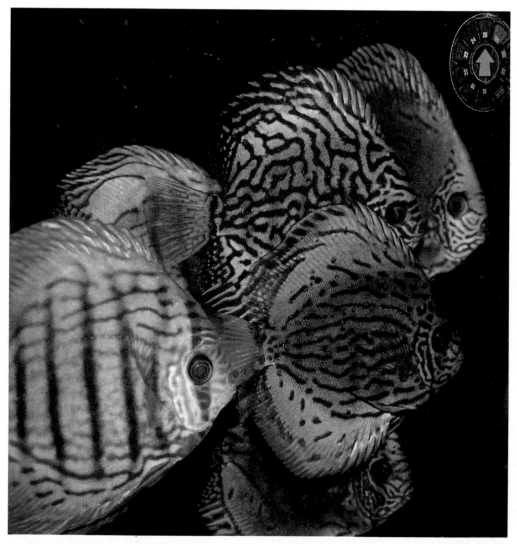

A variety of different turquoise discus kept together in a tank. These one year old specimens are congregating around a serving of their favourite discus food, specially developed by Tetra. In a shoal the competition for food is so keen that they will quickly adapt to any new food you may offer.

Ultimately, the sole criterion any discus fancier can apply when deciding whether or not to buy a particular fish, is its subjective aesthetic appeal. With young fish the question of colour markings is more difficult because the laws of heredity do not guarantee that the young of a solid coloured pair will turn out to be solid too. On the one hand you could certainly expect that the colouring of previous generations would show through however, and on the other, it can also be said that many young fish will continue to show brown stripes right through to the end of their growth at which point these may be covered over by a turquoise shade.

It would be wrong therefore to impute any suspicion of malpractice of a breeder offering ostensibly solid younsters that later only partially turn out as solid adults.

The colours that a discus displays are also very dependent upon its mood. As we know, discus are cichlids, that is to say, members of the perch family and as such have a heavy penchant for holding and defending their own territory. They start their tussles over territories when they are half-grown. In the course of these disputes subordinate individuals have a weaker basic colouring and all of the nine transverse stripes show up, whereas dominant specimens do not show their stripes and radiate the brightest of colours. Similarly, a pair involved in courtship display will show off their colours to the very best effect. A discus that is sick will turn dark, show its stripes and become quite timid. As one might expect, little of its former glory will be seen.

The time of day also has a bearing on the appearance of discus. In the morning,

immediately after the light is switched on, the fish are pale and the colour of their eyes is feeble. It is generally a good hour before they are seen in their full splendour. Feeding time often highlights the difference in colouring of the stronger and weaker individuals.

Nor should the lighting of the aquarium be forgotten in this context. The type of tube can have a dramatic effect on the colour of a discus with warm-toned lights being preferable. Grolux and Fluora lights influence the appearance. Grolux tubes emphasise the red shades whereas white tubes help bring out the best in the blue shades. It is really a matter for the individual hobbyist to set up the lighting to suit his personal preference. Even the lighting arrangement changes the colouring of discus so that you also have to decide whether you want to opt for front, top or back lighting. Your fish will look different depending on the incidence of the light. This is particularly noticeable in flashlight photographs. In one picture the fish might look green and in the next blue. This effect is caused by the angle of reflection of the light. For this reason it is a good idea to have a number of photos of your favourite fish so that at least one will show it at its best.

As it is very difficult to classify captive-bred discus into a typical colour variant category, in this book we will endeavour to give the right name of each colour variant with the illustrations.

A pair of brilliant turquoise discus. The lower fish, a female, still has a quite marked brown basic striping. This marking is receding in the male. With careful selective breeding this characteristic will gradually be suppressed until solid- coloured fish turn up in batches of youngsters.

Turquoise Discus

The fish referred to with this hybrid variant is an established collective term for discus fish that have turquoise- coloured longitudinal stripes on their body. One of the most prized features is that the whole body should be covered by the striping. The background colour of the body is brownish but the turquoise of the stripes should account for over 50 % of the body so that one could almost say that the blue shade ought to be considered as the ground colour with the brown being the stripes.

Brilliant Turquoise Discus

In this variant of the discus the breeders have succeeded in suppressing the brown of the ground colour even further so that it is reduced to the level of thin, fine lines. This gives the discus the appearance of being almost wholly blue. The blue colouring is so intense that it takes on an overall brilliance. To put it in even stronger terms, one might go so far as to say that it should have a metallic sheen.

Those specimens that do not have this high sheen should be traded as turquoise discus.

Red Turquoise Discus

This colour variant is difficult to identify with any degree of certainty. Unfortunately, many breeders like to see somewhat more red in their fish than is necessary. The colour red seems to have impressed itself upon the minds of many discus breeders, with a shade of tomato red apparently being some kind of Holy Grail. However, there are many beautiful red turquoise which are not such a strong shade of red and which could be classed as reddy-brown. The ideal red turquoise discus has intense reddy brown lines as the base colour and strong turquoise stripes. Depending on the strain, this turquoise striping may vary greatly in width.

The important factor is the deep reddish brown base colour.

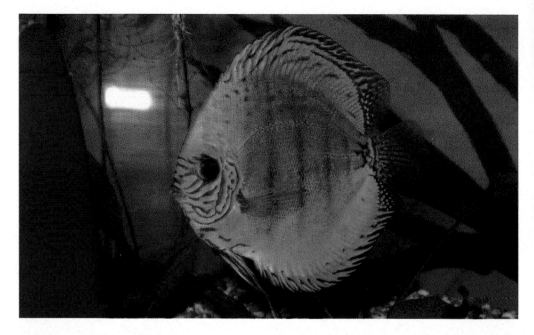

Solid Turquoise Discus

For many discus fanciers this is the most beautiful variant of all but, of course, not everybody shares the same tastes. Critics of this fish say that they find the uniform block of colour just too monotonous.

But judge for yourself. Solid turquoise discus should be lacking in any brown striping at all on their body. The only permissible striping is on the head. Its turquoise colouring runs across the whole of its body as far as the fins. On the hems of the fins delicate brown or red stripes are allowed.

Many breeders see their solid-coloured discus fish as having a true blue ground colour and are then inclined to use the title "Solid Cobalt Blue Discus". But as I have already stated, in a different light you may well see much more of the green shade shining through.

It is perhaps advisable to regard these four colour variants as the basic types. Any other names should be treated with a degree of caution. If an absolutely solid discus is crossed with a broad-striped red turquoise specimen, many of their progeny would certainly have a lovely turquoise colour with lots of reddy brown stripes or spots. But to start bandying around terms like "red-spotted turquoise" or "pearled red turquoise" would be presumptuous. A much more important factor than these whimsical colour sports is the health and conformation of the fish being raised. Any defects in form, striping or gill formation should be eradicated. Not every discus that can breed should be used for this purpose. And the responsibility for choosing the right stock lies with their keeper.

Through a strict selection process focussing on reddy coloured brown discus, it is possible to produce hybrids with genuinely red colouring. One could not say that such experiments have been a total success because the red strain is especially difficult to bring out.

A typical watery habitat near Manaus. The water is very cloudy and turbid as a result of the high levels of sediment carried by the rivers. This is particularly so during the rainy season when whole areas are inundated, as in this photograph. At such times fish will find copious supplies of food in the flood waters.

WILD-CAUGHT OR CAPTIVE-BRED?

This question is not as simple as it may sound since a lot depends on individual taste. Wild-caught discus are not as intensely coloured as turquoise discus though their colouring, while different, is still superb. A large, splendid green, wild-caught discus, with its delicate greenish-brown base colour and red flecks in the fin hem, or its broad turquoise stripes in the head region undoubtedly represents a good buy. On the other hand, the totally solid-coloured hybrid discus with its literally "spotless" block of colour and majestic presence is equally attractive in some people's eyes. Sometimes the decision can be excruciatingly difficult. In such cases the price can turn out to be the decisive factor because solid blue discus can often cost many times the price of a green wild-caught specimen.

Most dealers stock fish from both sources. If the fish on display are on the small side one can often assume that these are captive-bred because those specimens imported from Brazil are usually half- or even fully-grown. The offspring of wild-caught fish may also be available through the trade but are something of an exception. Captive-bred fish may originate from breeders' tanks in this country but large numbers of them arrive from sources in Asia. Over the years some Asiatic countries have proved reliable suppliers of very good stock.

As wild-caught discus come from a natural environment, they are likely to set higher requirements of their new owner in respect of water composition and diet. Their keeper will need to show a little more patience than is often the case with acclimatised captive-bred fish.

The latter are already used to eating a whole range of artificial food whereas wild-caught fish can often need some time initially to accustom themselves to the new diet. Wild-caught fish also need to recover from the rigours of their long journey, not to mention their periods of confinement in the nets of the catchers and the dealers' tanks. But if the dealer manages to rehabilitate them after their ordeal then the amateur fishkeeper can look forward to many years of pleasure from a wild-caught discus.

Clearly it is vital to try to ensure that you invest in a healthy discus. Therefore the potential buyer needs to know how to tell if a discus is healthy. In the first instance it has to be said that the overall impression counts for a lot. If you watch fish closely for a time you will appreciate that healthy specimens display a certain level of activity though it must be borne in mind that the discus is a rather placid type on the whole.

Individuals should have the typically round discus shape and under no circumstances should it give the impression of having a "stretched" body. The head parts must have a well-built look and, seen from the front, there must be no hint of a sunken forehead. The fish should have some "fat

A young, green, wild-caught discus that was about 12 cm long at the time of the photograph. The red dots on its side and on the lower fin hem can clearly be seen.

on its bones" and a concave belly is not a good sign. The eye must be a clear, strong colour though the question of whether or not red eyes are indispensable is surely a matter of personal taste.

In any event the size of the eye must be appropriate and proportional to the size of the body. Small fish with large eyes probably have growth defects. The discus fish that you buy must on no account be the sort of individual that sits in the corner of the tank looking dark and drab. If the fish are lively swimmers and showing their nine transverse stripes to good effect, then they are probably in good order.

White, gelatinous, slimy faeces in the aquarium is an indication of disease. If the discus are trailing round a white thread of faeces they are likely to be ill and nursing them back to health could prove a lengthy, laborious process.

Healthy discus have black or reddish-brown faeces. It will certainly be reddish-brown if they are fed on the new Tetra Discus food. If you have the chance of watching potential acquisitions feed, you can be assured that a healthy appetite is a sure sign of healthy fish. However, you should not transport freshly-fed fish as the water in a small transport container quickly becomes fouled. If they are to be shipped over a lengthy journey, these fish should not be fed for one or, better still, two days beforehand.

The buyer expects fine, colourful fish. However, young fish are no indication of the splendour that is to come under normal circumstances. If you do come across young discus that are already highly-coloured then you should consider the possibility that they may have been "doctored" by additions of hormones in their food or water. Reputable dealers would not, of course, resort to such practices because

A fish bred from green, wild-caught parents. At eight months old, this fish is already showing good colour features.

their trickery would soon be revealed when the fish lost their colour after a couple of weeks.

You would be well advised to take a close look at the gill covers of any prospective purchases because discus are often attacked by gill parasites. As a consequence, the fish can only breathe on one side due to one gill cover being stuck tightly closed while the other works overtime opening and shutting in a laboured fashion. Healthy fish breathe evenly and steadily through both gills. Bacterial gill infections can also make life difficult for discus. There are medicines that control these pests but an outbreak can prove stubborn and may require prolonged treatment. The medicine sold under the brand name Gyrotox® is available through petshops and is specifically indicated for the control of gill worms. However, this preparation must not be used in soft water. Like all medicines, the instructions should be carefully read and followed.

External fin damage in discus will rapidly be repaired by natural regrowth. It is quite normal for newly-imported wild-caught specimens to show signs of fin damage and you can be assured that this will be rectified through regeneration within a few days. So do not let yourself be put off buying a nice specimen on these grounds. The question of "disease prevention" is dealt with in a separate chapter of this book and further reading on the subject is indicated in the bibliography at the end of the work.

There are also some ground rules that should be followed when you are transporting discus. It is essential that these fish be carried in large double-skinned bags. Such large, powerful fish may easily perforate a single skin of their transit bags with the rays of their dorsal fin. In the case of extra large specimens it may be a wise precaution to provide a third bag.

They will withstand journeys of up to two hours without any need for additional supplies of pure oxygen. When they are likely to be in transit for longer than this, additional oxygen supplies should be made available through the medium of pure oxygen. So called oxygen tablets with a peroxide base should not be used because peroxide can attack the mucous membrane.

By adding pure oxygen at the outset you will not encounter any transport problems because bags that are half-filled with water and then topped up with oxygen are capable of supporting discus for 36 hours at the right temperature. Over such journeys the temperature may even be allowed to fall to as low as 20°C. When the fish are introduced to their new permanent home, care should be taken to increase the temperature gradually, changing the water in gentle stages.

This water exchange allows the pH and temperature of the two sets of water to reach a gradual equilibrium. If the procedure is carried out slowly over, say, a 30-minute period, the risk of any shock at the change of environment can be eliminated.

When first put into a new aquarium discus will often lie resting on the bottom or adopt a kind of diagonal posture. However, this behaviour quickly changes. You often see initially quite forlorn-looking discus cheerfully swimming around the tank an hour later, as if nothing had happened.

Large discus should not be fed on the day of their release into a new tank, though

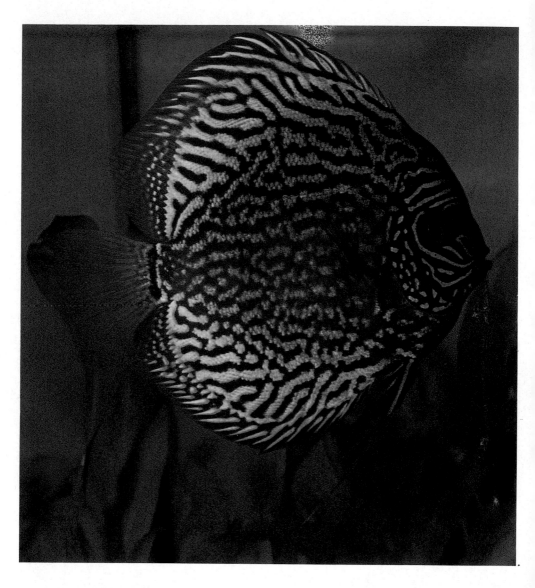

young fish will blithely carry on eating with a hearty appetite.

If you already have discus and are buying new ones to add to your collection, it is essential that you plan a proper period of quarantine for your new acquisitions. During this quarantine you will soon be able to determine whether the fish are healthy, eating well and otherwise showing normal behaviour. If you observe this procedure, you will have no problems with either wild-caught or captive-bred discus.

Setting up a discus aquarium

Perhaps the first question that needs to be addressed is: "Just what should the finished discus tank look like?" Indeed, it is a question that is not easily answered because it's a fact that the majority of discus aquaria are simply utilitarian Spartan affairs with little in the way of ground-covering, plants or decorative pieces of bogwood: in short very little of the very things that amateur fishkeepers hold so dear. So why have tanks with merely the bare essentials become more or less the norm? The main reason is simply the fact that they are easy to keep clean, because food scraps and other detritus can be siphoned off daily and with little bother. The matter of water changes is simplified and the discus are easier to keep under control.

Those fishkeepers who prefer this kind of discus tank doubtless intend to breed from their stock. However, this kind of discus breeding tank will be dealt with in another chapter.

The other type — and certainly the more appealing option — will be described here and constitutes the central purpose of this book.

Crossing a green wild-caught discus and a red turquoise specimen produced this beautifully marked female. Usually, long pectoral fins and the bullish head indicate a male but the rounded fin tips signal that it is indeed a female (p. 44).

The aquarium

As discus are large fish, this is obviously one of the fundamental considerations to be borne in mind when selecting the aquarium. The absolute minimum length for a discus tank is 100 cm, with a depth and width of 50 cm in each case being appropriate. Such a 250-litre capacity tank is adequate for a population of up to ten smallish discus or four half-grown specimens. A pair of fully grown discus would also feel at home here. When recommending this kind of stock level one is working on the assumption that other species of fish will be housed in the tank as well. In essence,

the basic rule on stocking aquaria holds, namely that the real art lies in keeping to the lower limits of what is possible. The bigger the aquarium, the easier it is to manage. Large tanks with a capacity of 500 litres and above require less maintenance work than small ones (which tend to become polluted quite quickly). The self-cleaning facility that tends to be established once a "biological balance" sets in is more easily achieved in a large tank.

If the discus aquarium is intended as a centre-piece in the home then its dimensions are clearly going to be dictated by circumstances. The first question is whether you should opt for an all-glass aquarium or a frame tank. It is a matter that is often decided on grounds of taste and, possibly, price. If you choose an all-glass aquarium make sure that the edges are ground to eliminate safety hazards and check that the thickness of the glass is adequate too. A wide range of quality tanks are available through the retail trade.

Positioning the aquarium

There may be a number of places that are suitable for locating an aquarium. However one location that can be ruled out immediately is in front of a window, because an aquarium that receives too much daylight will soon be presenting its owner with the problem of trying to keep rampant algal growth in check. A spot near to a door that is constantly being opened and shut cannot be recommended either because the fish may shown an adverse reaction to noise or sudden shadows. One factor that must be taken into consideration by any new aquarium owner is the weight of the aquarium. A 250-litre tank will weigh approximately 250 kg. This is of particular concern for people in rented accommodation, or with unstable flooring.

As an aquarium of these proportions cannot simply be placed on any old stand, it is advisable to acquire a robust support made of metal or strong wood. A polystyrene sheet one or two centimetres thick should be positioned under the bottom glass to take some of the weight. This polystyrene sheet is readily deformed under load and thus uneven stresses on the glass are absorbed. Without such a polystyrene

These two connected, octagonal aquaria make a really striking feature in a living-room. They are uncovered so that the plants can grow out over the top of the tanks.

Deep angelfish are very attractive fish but are unsuitable for keeping with discus.

sheet, cracks could easily occur in the bottom glass.

The trade has a wide range of complete aquarium systems on offer, including a variety of aquarium cabinets in different woods to suit the aquarium or indeed the room decor. It is important that the aquarium stands at least 70 centimetres above floor level so that the observer sitting relaxed in his easy chair can gain full benefit from his acquisition.

Once the aquarium has been set up in its final position, the back wall decoration should be put in place if this has not already been done. Such a decorative feature at the rear of the tank is a highly recommended, almost essential, part of the aquarium. There are printed backdrops available through the trade and adhesive films are also suitable. Dark backdrops are preferable, with dark blue, dark brown or even black proving suitable. Polystyrene sheets several centimetres thick can also be painted with anti-rust paint so that this preparation will then eat into the sheet to form crater-like depressions and create an interesting pattern. Once the paint has dried, these polystyrene sheets can be stuck on to the outside of the rear and side walls. There is no limit to the amount of invention that can go into aquarium decoration.

Part of an exemplary planting scheme in a discus aquarium. The numerous low-growing Echinodorus tenelus allow plenty of swimming room at the front of the tank.

Inside the tank natural backdrops can be created out of pieces of slate, roots or tall-growing plants. However, it is vital that you make sure that the items you use as decorative pieces do not contain any toxins or pollutants that will be released in the course of time. There must have been a number of instances when amateur fish-keepers have wondered why their charges looked so unwell and the answer has been a rotting root that has gradually been contaminating the whole aquarium.

Once the backdrop is in place you can set about installing the rest of the aquarium equipment and decoration.

Decoration

The planting of any aquarium is the real life-giving ingredient. Aquatic plants are an indispensable item in the discus aquarium too and as plants require nutrients, the first prerequisite is a suitable growing medium to cover the tank bottom. It must be said

that opinions as to the correct medium diverge widely. In an aquarium that is intended to house healthy discus, some kind of compromise has to be reached between the needs of the discus and those of the plants. A depth of 4 to 6 cm for the bed material is quite sufficient. One of the very best media has proved to be dark gravel with a grain size of 4 to 8 mm, mixed with coarse sand from 1 to 3 mm. Small amounts of plant nutrients can be mixed into this. Under no circumstances should any garden soil be put into the tank. It goes without saying that the sand and gravel mixture should have been thoroughly washed prior to use.

Small terrace-like structures can be built using lime-free rocks such as slate. Once the rock features are in place, suitable aquatic plants can be planted in the substrate, always taking care not to bend the roots. The root ends should be trimmed before planting and the plants should be pressed down firmly into the gravel mixture. When adding water to the aquarium an upturned saucer or plate should be placed in one of the open areas on the gravel to deflect the jet of inflowing water and thus prevent the gravel being washed away. If the water is put into the tank at a slow steady rate it will remain more or less clear. Fill the tank to three quarters of its ultimate depth and then put in the rest of the decorative material. This may include a number of fine, attractive stones or rocks but, as already noted, they must be of the type that will not release any lime into the water. In order to verify that they are lime-free, all you need do is pour a drop of dilute hydrochloric acid on to the stone. If the rock starts to foam, then it contains lime and is unsuitable.

Roots are also a nice decorative material though you are advised to exercise some caution here. Only use those roots that are hard and not rotten. Genuine bogwood roots, Argentinian savannah roots, Scottish peat bog oak or xylolite are all suitable. If the water starts to smell fusty then the root should be removed. If possible you should then brush it off vigorously in hot water and rinse it in several changes of water. Some types of wood float, while others, like xylolite or Argentinian savannah wood are immediately submerged.

Roots with a strong tendency to float must be secured in place using rubber suction cups or fishing line. When the items of decoration and aquatic plants are in the right place the rest of the water can be put in.

Lighting

Light is of the utmost importance for the photosynthesis of plants.

The question of copying natural light patterns is and remains a very patchy business. In the tropics the rhythm of night and day is quite different from Europe, with a dawn and dusk twilight phase that is very short. Night falls very suddenly. At about six in the evening it gets dark in the space of just a few minutes. One minute the sun is shining and the next you cannot see your hand in front of your face, with the process being reversed at dawn. The tropical day unfolds in a precise 12-hour rhythm and the plants that come from these regions thrive best on twelve hours of illumination.

The principal medium used for illumination these days is the fluorescent tube. Various colours can be used in combination.

Generally speaking, discus are kept in darkish aquaria, a custom that is supposed to reflect the fact that they shy away from light in their home waters and seem to prefer dark waters. It is, of course, a misconception since discus seem to be as much at home in well-lit aquaria as any other fish.

Timid behaviour in discus can often be attributed to diffused light. In order to increase the light yield, a reflector should be fitted over the lamp. It should also be borne in mind that fluorescent tubes lose up to 50 % of their power after as little as six months so that regular tube changes are advisable.

An alternative to fluorescent tubes are mercury vapour or metalhalide spot lamps that are often very effective means of lighting open tanks. These powerful lamps will in most cases guarantee good plant growth.

A fluorescent tube housed
in an aquarium cover.

If the water is more than
60 cm deep, mercury
vapour lamps are needed.

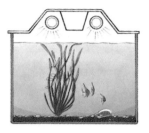

Two or more fluorescent
tubes are required for
larger tanks.

Heating

The discus aquarium must have some form
of artificial heating. In their natural habitat
discus live in waters that have an average
temperature of around 30 °C. This high
temperature is irreconcilable with many
types of aquatic plants and so temperatures
of about 27 °C should be regarded as the
best guideline figure. As the discus tank
will normally stand in a lounge which is in
any case going to be heated, in principle,
any normal size of additional heating will
suffice. The customary method of heating
is the thermostat-controlled heating element. This kind of device can be set at the
desired temperature and will then keep at
this constant level in a very reliable fashion.
For aquaria in heated living rooms a heating capacity of one Watt of heating output

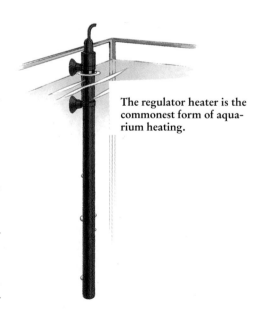

The regulator heater is the
commonest form of aqua-
rium heating.

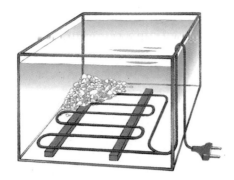

Heating cables are laid out in loops on the aquarium bed.

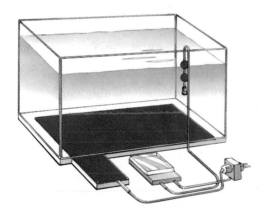

The heating mat is placed under the aquarium. The water is heated from below, creating a natural circulation as the heat rises.

per two litres of water is quite adequate. Another method of heating an aquarium is to lay heating cables in the substrate material or to use a heating plate. Temperature sensors with highly accurate thermostats are now available to guarantee that any

temperature fluctuations will be kept to the very minimum.

If an aquarium is boldly lit and the coils of the fluorescent tubes are housed in the enclosed aquarium cabinet, then it should be borne in mind that the latter also give off a lot of heat. This means in effect that the aquarium heating can be designed to operate at even lower levels.

Filtration

Every aquarium needs a filtration system. Every aquarist knows this, but what is the precise function of the aquarium filter? Primarily, it is there to provide clean water, but in a good aquarium filter there are a number of biological processes constantly taking place. Bacteria colonise the filter material and so play an additional role in breaking down harmful substances. By using a variety of filter media the pH value and water composition can also be influenced and changed. A modern aquarium filter is so much more than just a basic tool for keeping water looking clear.

Essentially, one has to differentiate between the three basic types of filtration, namely mechanical, chemical and biological filtration.

With mechanically or chemically based filters the water is forced through boxes filled with filter material. Filters that operate on a biological basis work with porous filter material which has been colonised by bacteria and it is these that undertake the task of breaking down pollutants and other harmful substances.

The aquarist will also probably be asking himself whether to opt for an internal or external system. With a cabinet-mounted aquarium an external filter makes much more sense. After all, internal filters somehow always manage to remain visible despite our efforts and impair the overall visual effect. Internal filters are ideal for breeding tanks and smaller raising tanks. For this reason this kind of filter will be dealt with in greater depth later on in the book.

Furthermore, it is necessary to distinguish between the two different types of external filter. On the one hand there are open external filters that either hang outside or stand next to the aquarium. This system comprises a glass or plastic box that contains various filter chambers which in turn hold the actual substrate for the filtration process. The water is siphoned off through an overflow tube, passed through the filter and then, on the other side, pumped back into the aquarium by air or by an electrical pump. The overall design plan for an aquarium should take due account of the need to accommodate such a filtration system.

The second group of external filters includes the electrically-driven pot filters. These are excellent systems consisting of a large filter pot with its own motor mounted above. It has one tube that sucks water out of the aquarium and a second that returns the water to the tank after cleaning in the filter. These external filters have the advantage that they can conveniently be placed under the aquarium so that it is easy to house them in the aquarium cabinet itself.

The filtering effect of both types of external filter is determined by the actual filter medium used in each case. Filter pads

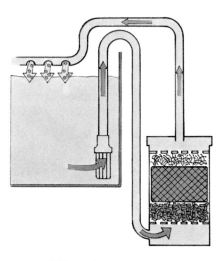

External filters do not need to be cleaned so frequently as they possess a greater filtering capacity. This means that the fish are not disturbed so often.

have proved themselves to be a very effective pre-filtering material. They quickly remove any coarse contaminants and are easy to change. Aquarium grade peat as a filter medium has a mild softening effect on the water and also acidifies it slightly, making it ideal for use in the discus aquarium. Clay pipes or gravel are also suitable as coarse filters in external systems though you must ensure that this type of filter material does not leach any lime into the water.

The use of active charcoal is recommended in those instances where you want to alter the state of the water. Active charcoal has the capacity to filter out and remove residues of medicinal preparations and other compounds. If the aquarium water starts to take on an unwanted yellowish hue, there are special sorts of active

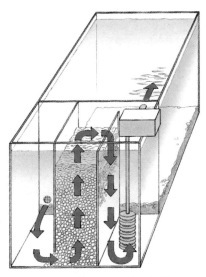

This is an excellent example of a filter that has been built into the tank.

charcoal that will filter out this unwanted colour.

The use of artificial resins for filtration purposes will be dealt with in a subsequent chapter.

Let us now take a look at the biological/bacterial method of filtration. In the last few years the efficiency of a biological (or bio-) filter has been recognised so that there are now many aquarium set-ups that are being run with large biological filters.

These large filter chambers are often self-built affairs. In this method of filtration aerobic bacteria — which is to say those that require oxygen in order to function — take over the degradation processes in the aquarium. Sponge filters such as the Tetra Brillant-Filter are probably the simplest and certainly very effective biofilters because many bacteria can colonise these foam sponges and take on the job of breaking down fish waste. For this reason you should never clean foam cartridges with excessively hot or cold water. Cleaning should be carried out in warm water with a temperature of about 25 °C so as not to harm the bacteria. Sponges cleaned in this way will be able to return to their full cleaning duties immediately. These sponge filters are particularly well suited for use in the discus breeding tank.

The aerobic bacteria of a biofilter need a constant supply of oxygen and they should always be offered a very porous filter material with a large surface area to colonise. The water should flow through the filter material at a high rate so that the bacteria receive sufficient oxygen to function effectively. Alternative biological filters are occasionally used by discus keepers under the general name of trickle filters. The basic principle used here is similar to the trickle or drip technique commonly employed in sewage or water-treatment plants. The bacteria that have colonised the porous filter material feed on the products that result from the metabolic processes taking place in the aquarium. The bacteria break down toxic substances such as ammonium compounds, using a three-stage procedure that results in less harmful substances. Ammonium arises in the aquarium from

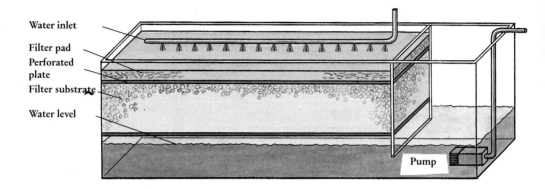

Water inlet
Filter pad
Perforated plate
Filter substrate
Water level
Pump

Aerobic bacteria colonise the filter substrate to break down any pollutants in this scrubbing filter.

activities like gill respiration of the fish and through the bacterial changes in their faeces. Nitrosomas bacteria convert ammonium into nitrite. This nitrite is in turn converted into nitrate by nitrification bacteria. Nitrite and ammonium are both toxic to fish and so need to be converted into harmless nitrate which can then be absorbed by plants in the water. But nitrate can also be reduced by simply carrying out partial water changes. Excessively high concentrations of nitrate are not tolerated by discus and they will not thrive under such conditions.

If at all possible, the nitrate content should not exceed 50 mg/l. Nitrate measurement kits are available through dealers. But to return to our discus aquarium in the living room: it has been set out with the appropriate type of bed material, suitable decorative features and a nice selection of plants. The heating system is providing a steady temperature of 27 °C and the filter is running smoothly and efficiently ... so it's time to put the fish in. Or is it? In fact, now is the time to exercise a

little patience. Check that the water quality is right: the pH value should have settled at between 6.0 and 7.0; the hardness should not be too high. If it is, it must first be softened. Some important points on this aspect are discussed in the chapter on "The Art of Discus Breeding".

It would be ideal if the plants could be given a little time to start growing. Since it is quite common for algae to flourish when an aquarium is newly set up, a number of algae-eating fish species should be introduced into the tank, such as Ancitrus catfish, platies, or Crossocheilus siamensis or Gyrinocheilus aymonieri from Thailand. If these reputable algae-eaters are put in at the outset and not fed at all for the first couple of weeks, they will soon eliminate any chance of the algae gaining a foothold in the tank. After a week or two the aquarium will have settled down somewhat and you can start thinking about introducing your discus and their companions. Suitable species for accompanying the languid discus are mentioned in a separate chapter.

THE RIGHT PLANTS

In reality discus and aquatic plants are something of a mismatch. In their natural habitat in Amazonas, discus do not encounter or rely on any particular vegetation. But as the majority of us do not want to be without some fine, healthy greenery in our aquarium, we need to know which are the most suitable plants. High water temperatures and soft, acidic water are not ideal conditions for many aquatic plants. And yet these are the ideal conditions for discus. However, there are some plants which are not found in Amazonas but which are suited to the conditions found there. For example, plants from Asia have proved useful in discus aquaria simply because they are more durable in this potentially inhospitable environment. The selection of plants from alternative environments is usually necessary because a biotope aquarium does not meet most people's aesthetic sensibilities. So the primary aim of this chapter is to give some solid, practical guidelines.

A shoal of fully-grown wild-caught, green discus, looking very much at home in this established aquarium.

Plants make a vital contribution to keeping an aquarium healthy. In a tank that contains lots of flourishing plants you will find that the level of disease amongst the fish population is reduced. After all, good plant growth is a sure sign of a sound bio-rhythm. Healthy, luxuriant plants help eradicate whole quantities of the various minerals that can be harmful for discus, including nitrate. In turn, a properly functioning aquarium with a good stock of fish produces many of the nutrients that plants require. The plants give off substantial amounts of oxygen that the fish need. The most important nutrient that plants require is carbon dioxide (CO_2). If the plants' metabolic rate is high at any given time, they will consume a lot of CO_2 and a deficit will ensue. This deficit can be compensated by using the Tetra CO_2 Supply Kit. This enhanced supply of CO_2 will induce them to put on stronger growth. It should also be mentioned here that as well as requiring extra CO_2, plants also need a supply of iron through fertilizers. The "light factor" has also been mentioned already in this context and it should be emphasised that plants cannot possibly thrive without adequate light. At least a half a Watt of light output should be provided for every litre of aquarium water which means that a 200-litre aquarium should be fitted with three fluorescent tubes each rated at 30 Watts.

Setting out plants in an aquarium involves a great deal of personal intuition and no amount of guidelines can replace this "knack". The plants recommended for a discus aquarium here have been selected so that any combination of planting schemes is possible.

There are some ground rules that should be borne in mind right at the out-set, ie when setting out the plants:
— Cut back any rotten leaves to healthy growth;
— Remove any blackened roots;
— Trim back the roots slightly;
— In group planting schemes leave sufficient space between plants;
— Set out rooted plants so that the crown just protrudes above the surface of the substrate;
— Make sure tuberous plants are planted right side up and not completely covered by gravel;
— Wrap bulbous plants in some thin foam sheet or a filter pad before planting out.

Under no circumstances should plants be set out at random in the aquarium. Well beforehand you should draw up a planting scheme perhaps on a scale of 1:10. Here the plants can be sketched in accordance with their ultimate growing height. Tall growing background plants should be used to conceal filter tubes, heating equipment or cables. Medium-sized plants look good nestling amongst bogwood roots and, of course, certain low-growing Amazonian species lend themselves perfectly to producing a lovely lawn effect at the front of the tank.

Any rampant growers must be regularly thinned. This kind of work is best done when carrying out the regular water changes.

Name	**Small-leaved Amazonian Sword Plant** *Echinodorus amazonicus*
Origin	Tropical South America
Height	Up to about 60 cm Lance-shaped leaves
Water quality	Soft to medium hard Temperature 20 to 30 °C
General care	A typical specimen plant that is easy to grow. Forms strong leaves if given CO_2 fertilizer.
Useful hints	A superb plant with light green leaves. Very tall growth so requires an aquarium of appropriate size. Very suitable for discus display aquaria. Requires a lot of light and will form adventitious plants on the flowering stem. Likes a nutritious growing medium and CO_2 fertilizer. Well-grown display specimens have dozens of leaves. Tough and hardy.

Name	**Dark-leaved Amazonian Sword Plant** *Echinodorus opacus*
Origin	Southern Brazil
Height	10 to 20 cm, leaves about 10 cm long and 4 — 6 cm wide
Water quality	Soft to medium hard Temperature 20 to 28 °C
General care	Easily grown and a suitable subject for shallower tanks. Fertilizer levels important.
Useful hints	A low-growing water plantain type species. Ideal for planting in the middle ground of a discus aquarium. Ceases growing for some time after replanting. Propagation through division of rhizomes.

Name	**Red-leaved Amazonian Sword Plant** *Echinodorus osiris*
Origin	Brazil
Height	Up to 60 cm Lance-shaped leaves up to 60 cm long
Water quality	Soft to medium hard Temperature 20 to 28 °C
General care	Requires good lighting. Best as a single specimen plant.
Useful hints	Used as a single specimen plant, this tall-growing Sword Plant can form an imposing focal point in a deep aquarium. The young leaves have a nice, reddish-brown colour. It can be propagated via the adventitious plantlets that form on the flower stems. These need a lot of light if they are to do well. It is very similar to the Small-leaved Amazonian Sword Plant that requires identical care.

Name	**Black Amazonian Sword Plant** *Echinodorus parviflorus*
Origin	Tropical South America
Height	Up to 25 cm approx.
Water quality	Soft to medium hard Temperature 22 to 28 °C
General care	A very adaptable plant. Recommended as a group plant in the discus aquarium.
Useful hints	A medium-sized plant that is also sold under the name Echinodorus peruensis. A beautiful plant seen at its best in small groups where it can form a good middle ground subject. Adapts readily to the lower light levels sometimes found in discus aquaria. In some ways an ideal plant thanks to the wide range of temperatures it will tolerate.

Name	**Black Amazonian Sword Plant,** var. "Tropica" *Echinodorus parviflorus Tropica*
Origin	Unknown
Height	Medium, up to 20 cm Leaf blade ovate or oval
Water quality	Soft to medium hard Temperature 22 to 28 °C
General care	This species grows well. A nice group plant for larger discus aquaria.
Useful hints	A deep green plant and a real pleasure to look at. A very good grower, frequently on offer in aquatic shops. Several plants should be set out in groups. Will adapt to the light available, though the shape of the leaf will be somewhat rounded if light levels are low. Will tolerate temperatures up to 30 °C.

Name	**Dwarf Amazonian Sword Plant** *Echinodorus quadricostatus*
Origin	Brazil
Height	In the aquarium up to 20 cm. Lanceolate leaves up to 15 cm
Water quality	Soft to medium hard Temperature 22 to 28 °C
General care	An easily kept species. Requires additions of iron fertilizers.
Useful hints	An ideal decorative plant for the foreground. Variable growth habit from five to twenty-five centimetres. Propagates itself quickly and readily through runners, so it should not be planted too densely at the outset. Requires frequent thinning and total replanting occasionally. Quickly shows an adverse reaction to a shortage of iron by yellowing of leaves. Very adaptable to the prevailing light conditions. Thoroughly recommended plant for the discus aquarium.

Name	**Pygmy Chain Amazon Sword Plant** *Echinodorus tenellus*
Origin	Central and South America
Height	Up to 10 cm Thin grasslike leaves
Water quality	Soft to medium hard Temperature 22 to 28 °C
General care	Easy to grow if the lighting is good. A foreground subject that forms a lawn-like cover.
Useful hints	In appearance it is more reminiscent of a Sagittaria than an Echinodorus. The thin leaves usually only grow to 5 cm in length. Propagates profusely through runners. A carpet plant that is very decorative when planted at the front of an aquarium. Where the light is insufficient growth may suffer.

Name	**Wavy Sword Plant** *Aponogeton boivinianus*
Origin	Madagascar
Height	Up to 50 cm. Narrow, heavily crimped leaves
General care	A rampant grower that needs a rest period.
Useful hints	A very beautiful species of Aponogeton that is particularly well suited to large aquaria. It forms a wealth of deeply coloured, crimped leaves. A popular subject sold by many stockists. After a period of vigorous leaf growth and flowering, the plant is likely to lose some of its vitality. At this point the plant needs a rest period outside the aquarium. If bedded in earth and kept slightly moist, the tuber can be replanted in the aquarium some two to four months later where it will immediately start to throw out new leaves.

Ruffled Sword Plant Aponogeton crispus (Syn. *Aponogeton echinatus*)
Origin: Sri Lanka and India
Height: 30 cm long leaves
General care: Needs regular rest periods

Useful hints: This wavy-leafed plant is a light or deep green colour and is often listed by dealers. Planted in groups, they look good in the middle of a discus aquarium.

67

Name	**Tiger Lotus** *Nymphaea lotus (photo above and right)*
Origin	Tropical Africa
Height	Up to 20 cm Also throws out floating leaves
Water quality	Soft to hard Temperature 22 to 28 °C
General care	A very durable and decorative aquarium plant. High light requirement.
Useful hints	One of the most beautiful aquarium plants that is available in both a red and green form. A typical specimen plant. Fully grown plants send out floating leaves. If these are not wanted they can simply be broken off. The plant will then produce short-stemmed leaves to replace them. If grown together with floating plants, it will produce blooms that open at night. It is possible to propagate them from offsets that form on runners.

Name	**Common Eel Grass** *Vallisneria spiralis*
Origin	Tropical and sub-tropical regions
Height	Up to 50 cm Narrow, twisted leaves
Water quality	Soft to hard Temperature 20 to 30 °C
General care	A durable, decorative plant that can survive in soft water but thrives best in harder water types.
Useful hints	One of several species of the popular Vallisnerias. Very decorative at the rear of the tank. With its abundant runners it soon forms a dense tangle of growth. Prefers good light, though it will also grow under weaker light conditions, albeit more slowly. The taller growing types of Vallisneria are really tailor-made for the discus aquarium as the thickets that are formed are ideal for concealing the heater, cables and tubes.

Name	**Java Fern** *Microsorium pteropus*
Origin	South East Asia
Height	Up to 20 cm long, mid to dark green leaves
Water quality	Soft to medium hard Temperature 20 to 30 °C
General care	This plant typically lends itself to being attached to bogwood or rocks. Durable and slow growing.
Useful hints	It can be planted out but this is not recommended as the real strength of this plant lies in its capacity to thrive on bogwood or stone. Adapts to any aquarium lighting.

Name	**Giant Ambulia** *Limnophila aquatica*
Origin	Sri Lanka
Height	Up to 50 cm in the aquarium The large whorls of leaves have a diameter of up to 10 cm
Water quality	Soft to medium hard Temperature 20 to 28 °C
General care	Needs very good lighting. 28 °C is the absolute upper temperature limit.
Useful hints	A very decorative plant, seen to best effect planted in groups in large tanks. Has a branching growth habit and can be propagated by breaking off these arms for use as cuttings. Likes frequent water changes. Can require some length of time to settle down. Essential that it has a well-lit position in the aquarium.

Name	**Cryptocoryne crispatula**
Origin	Thailand, Indo China
Height	Up to 50 cm. Very wavy, crinkled leaves that can grow to 40 to 50 cm in length
Water quality	Medium hard to hard Temperature 22 to 28 °C
General care	Not at all fussy about lighting. Partial water changes help promote good growth.
Useful hints	The crinkled leaves make a very decorative show when planted in groups. May well be found under the old name of Cryptocoryne balansae. This Cryptocoryne is very undemanding and thrives almost anywhere.

Name	**Wendt's Cryptocoryne** *Cryptocoryne wendtii* (Brown form)
Origin	Sri Lanka
Height	10 to 20 cm Brown form
Water quality	Soft to medium hard Temperature 22 to 28 °C
General care	See notes on green form (next page).
Useful hints	This brown colour variant has the same requirements as the green form (next page). Highly recommended for the fore-ground or the middle of the tank.

Name	**Wendt's Cryptocoryne** *Cryptocoryne wendtii* (Green form)
Origin	Sri Lanka
Height	10 to 20 cm Green form
Water quality	Soft to medium hard Temperature 22 to 28 °C
General care	An undemanding plant that will make do with a moderate level of lighting.
Useful hints	This cryptocoryne is also to be recommended for the discus aquarium. This species does not grow too tall and so is suited to the middle part of the tank. As a species Wendt's Cryptocoryne has a large number of forms, with various colours available through the trade. Their general care is the same. The individual variants are difficult to tell apart and hard to identify with any certainty.

Name	**Water hyacinth** *Eichhornia crassipes*
Origin	Tropical South America, but now found in many parts of the world
Height	Diameter 10 to 15 cm but can grow larger
Water quality	Soft to medium hard Temperature 22 to 30 °C
General care	A floating plant that requires very good lighting.
Useful hints	Provides an easy cover for a discus aquarium. Totally undemanding except for high light requirement. Propagation through runners.

COMPATIBLE SPECIES OF FISH

Once your discus aquarium has been set up — and it is almost certain to be of a bigger size than the average tank — it will soon become apparent that there is going to be enough room there for some other fish. There is no doubt that other fish can be kept with discus, but a certain amount of care and thought has to be exercised to ensure that their lifestyles are compatible.

The question often arises as to whether scalares make suitable companions for discus and, unfortunately, the answer is a categorical no. The reason is not only the risk of their passing on disease but also the feeding habits of scalares. They are simply too greedy. The discus will lose out in the competition for food and soon show signs of ailing. The placid discus fish should

Scalares in a planted tank are a breathtakingly beautiful picture but for all that, discus fans should resist the temptation of keeping these two species together as scalares can transmit "hole in the head" disease. Moreover, scalares are voracious eaters and easily outdo discus when it comes to competing for food.

A turquoise discus in a nicely-planted aquarium. This magnificent specimen shows all the characteristics of a male.

therefore only be kept in the company of equally peaceable subjects. Algae eaters have already been mentioned in the chapter on setting up the aquarium and may be left in the tank. Smaller characins, particularly shoalers, also enliven the scene. Quite clearly though, not all the characins recom-

mended in this book should be kept together in one and the same aquarium but two or three different shoals will do nicely in a large display tank.

Characins should never be kept as single specimens, as in this respect they are akin to discus which are a sociable species themselves. Smaller species of characin, like neon tetras, only look their best when swimming around in shoals of twenty to thirty fish when their colours can be seen to full advantage. Slightly larger characins are effective in shoals of just ten or so.

Large cichlids from South America, which ought to be suitable if the original

In the rainforests one frequently comes across little watercourses and sumps of left-over floodwater that are the habitat of various species of cichlids and catfish.

biotope is anything to go by, are not suitable for a discus community tank. Large cichlids are very territorial and would relentlessly pressurize the discus. So much so, in fact, that the discus would scarcely be seen during the spawning periods of the cichlids.

Dwarf cichlids on the other hand can be considered as suitable partners for discus. As they remain quite small and are generally peaceable, they are hardly likely to overpower the discus. But on no account should too many pairs of these be put in the tank either. In a discus tank of minimum size, of say 250 litres, one pair of dwarf cichlids can be put in per 100 litres of water.

The more placid catfish are ideal companions, especially the smaller Corydoras species. They spend their time tidying up the floor of the tank, hoovering up all the food scraps and generally acting like some kind of sanitary inspectorate. Nor do they compete with the discus in any way since they are more than content with the scraps from their table.

The species of Corydoras that are chosen must be a matter for the taste of the individual fish keeper because all of them are equally well-suited. As far as occupancy is concerned, the same rule of thumb applies as for dwarf cichlids.

Ancistrus catfish are good algae controllers and are happy to spend their entire day scraping away the algal growth on the aquarium glass. They will also scour the bottom for anything remotely edible. They are also worth their place in the sanitary inspectorate team.

Large, fully-grown indidivuals may be tempted to focus their attentions on a clutch of discus eggs but any discus pair worth their salt would see them off. So one should not really have any misgivings about introducing a pair or two of Ancistrus catfish.

Some of the larger species of catfish are less suitable because their nocturnal activities disturb the beauty sleep of the discus.

The three fish families recommended above will guarantee plenty of interest as companions to the star turns.

The following pages describe a wide range of species that can safely accompany discus. Of course this selection is not intended to be restrictive or binding but more as an aid to the aquarist who wants to eliminate mistakes at source.

Name	**Silver-tipped tetra** *Plasemania nana*
Origin	Eastern and western Brazil The smaller rivers of Amazonia
Maximum size	5 cm
General care	Shoaling fish, easy to keep.
Water quality	Soft to medium hard Temperature 24 to 28 °C
Sexual differences	Males are more highly-coloured, especially in the caudal fin, and have a slimmer body form.
Useful hints	Peaceable, very durable and a lively swimmer. Not at all choosy when it comes to food. Prefers a slightly acidic water.

Name	**Rummy-nose tetra** *Hemigrammus bleheri*
Origin	South America Upper reaches of the Amazon
Maximum size	5—8 cm
General care	Medium life span. Likes slightly acidic water. A peaceable shoaling fish.
Water quality	Soft to medium hard with additions of peat Temperature 24 to 28 °C
Sexual differences	Males have stronger colouring in the caudal fin and have a slimmer body form.
Useful hints	A peaceable shoaling fish that looks very attractive with its intensely red-coloured head. Its vivid colours will enhance any aquarium. Easily confused with the red-nosed tetra. Young are somewhat delicate but otherwise durable in soft, acidic water. Omnivorous.

Name	**Ornate (Bentos) tetra** *Hyphessobrycon bentosi bentosi*
Origin	Guayana and upper reaches of the Amazon
Maximum size	up to 4 cm
General care	Shoaling fish, easy to keep. Not at all fussy about water conditions.
Water quality	Soft to medium hard Temperature 24 to 30 °C
Sexual differences	Males have a flaglike, pronounced elongation to their dorsal fin. Slimmer, more streamlined in the belly region.
Useful hints	A beautiful, peaceable shoaling fish. At least 10 should be kept in a shoal. Ideal for the community tank. Keeps to the middle and lower water strata. Frequently sold in the trade. An omnivorous fish that is undemanding in terms of its water and food.

Name	**Bleeding heart tetra** *Hyphessobrycon erythrostigma*
Origin	Colombia
Maximum size	5 cm
General care	A very durable species that needs a high grade diet.
Water quality	Soft to medium hard Temperature 24 to 28 °C
Sexual differences	Fins on the males are much more elongated, especially the dorsal fin which extends behind it like a banner.
Useful hints	A magnificently coloured tetra which should be kept in a shoal. Single specimens will pine away. Unfortunately, not readily available. Shows its best colours when fed on a high grade diet with some animal content.

Name	**Black neon** *Hyphessobrycon herbertaxelrodi*
Origin	Amazon basin
Maximum size	4 cm
General care	Easy to keep because it has no special water requirements.
Water quality	Soft to medium hard Temperature 22 to 28 °C
Sexual differences	Females have rounder bellies and are generally fuller in appearance. Males sometimes have bluish white fin tips.
Useful hints	A peaceable shoaling fish that is constantly on the move. Swims in the upper half of the aquarium. Needs good, varied diet with some animal content. Tetra FD-Menu, for instance, is to be recommended.

Name	**Tube-mouthed Pencilfish** *Nannobrycon eques*
Origin	Amazonia, Rio Negro, Guayana
Maximum size	5 cm
General care	Not to be kept in the company of very lively fish. Crepuscular in habit.
Water quality	Soft, slightly acidic Temperature 22 to 28 °C
Sexual differences	Can be difficult to distinguish. Females are rather stocky with a rounder, fuller belly.
Useful hints	One of the more difficult subjects because it is sensitive to water quality. It requires fine food with some animal content. This is searched for mainly in the half-light. Should be kept in a shoal. Likes to hide in dense groups of plants.

Name	**Cardinal tetra** *Paracheirodon axelrodi*
Origin	Amazonas, northern tributaries of the Rio Negro
Maximum size	4 cm
General care	This species is easy to keep because it has no special requirements either in terms of water quality or food.
Water quality	Soft to medium hard Temperature 22 to 30 °C
Sexual differences	Difficult to differentiate. Males are somewhat slimmer.
Useful hints	A peaceful shoaling fish that is well-known and enjoys a good degree of popularity. Very intense colours that show up particularly well in aquaria with a dark decor. As little dots of colour they are a must for every discus aquarium. Likes a slightly acidic water that should be filtered over some peat. Omnivorous. Very difficult to breed.

Name	**Neon Tetra** *Paracheirodon innesi*
Origin	Eastern Peru, Rio Putumayo
Maximum size	4 cm
General care	Simple to keep; like the black neon, it does not have any major water requirements.
Water quality	Soft to hard Temperature 20 to 28 °C
Sexual differences	Males are slimmer than the fatter-bellied females.
Useful hints	Nowadays the most popular aquarium fish of all. Captive-bred specimens are very undemanding. In the wild it is a lover of soft, acidic water. All in all it is an ideal discus companion fish. Essential that it is kept in a shoal. In a large aquarium you can safely put in 50 to 100 of them. Eats any kind of finely-ground food.

Name	**X-ray tetra** *Pristella maxillaris*
Origin	Northern South America, Amazonas region
Maximum size	4 to 5 cm
General care	This species is easy to keep and is particularly at home in slightly acidic, very soft water.
Water quality	Soft water with added peat Temperature 22 to 28 °C
Sexual differences	Males are slimmer and their swim bladder which "shines through" this almost transparent fish, tails off to a point. In the female this is round. The caudal fin coloration is stronger in the male.
Useful hints	A peaceable and undemanding shoal fish that shows off its best colours in very soft water. The colouring is very dependent on water quality and good food. This is a very active fish that needs an appropriate amount of free swimming room.

Name	**Penguin fish** *Thayeria boehlkei*
Origin	Amazonas basin, Peru
Maximum size	5 to 6 cm
General care	An undemanding fish which is, however, sensitive to high nitrate levels.
Water quality	Soft to medium hard Temperature 22 to 28 °C
Sexual differences	Males slimmer, females have a fuller-looking belly.
Useful hints	A calm, peaceful shoaling fish, ideal for the community tank. Likes regular, partial water changes. Captive-bred specimens tolerate higher water hardness levels. The discus aquarium is ideal for this tetra. Omnivorous and not at all fussy about food.

Name	**Agassiz' dwarf cichlid** *Apistogramma agassizii*
Origin	Brazil, Amazonas region
Maximum size	8 cm
General care	Easily kept in low-nitrate water. Strong territorial instinct.
Water quality	Soft to medium hard with added peat, slightly acidic Temperature 22 to 28 °C
Sexual differences	Easily differentiated. Males are larger and more colourful with elongated fin tips.
Useful hints	A peaceable dwarf cichlid that forms a territory. Not a digger. The male spawns with one female after another. Females care for the brood. Likes to hide out under roots. Spawns in cavities. Interesting brood care. Many colour variants are available.

Name	**Borelli's dwarf cichlid** *Apistogramma borellii*
Origin	South America, the Mato Grosso region
Maximum size	Males 8 cm, females 5 cm
General care	If water quality is right, easy to keep. Susceptible to use of medicines.
Water quality	Soft to medium hard with added peat Temperature 22 to 28 °C
Sexual differences	Males considerably bigger and more beautifully coloured. Fins more elongated
Useful hints	Peaceable dwarf cichlids. Males collect a harem. Subordinate males wear the paler colours of the females to help them hide away, so you should buy at least two females for every male. Spawning behaviour as for A. agassizii. They eat live food, freeze-dried food and the special discus food, once they have settled in.

Name	Ram *Papiliochromis ramirezi*
Origin	Savanna country, west of the Rio Orinoco in Venezuela and Colombia
Maximum size	5 to 7 cm
General care	A good fish to keep together with quiet species. Territorial.
Water quality	Soft, though captive-bred specimens can cope with medium hard. Temperature 22 to 30 °C
Sexual differences	Males are somewhat larger and better-coloured. Third and fourth dorsal fin ray more elongated.
Useful hints	In aquaria with placid fish it feels at home in small groups. Excavates spawning holes. Difficult to induce to breed under natural conditions and some artificial aids are generally used. A very popular aquarium fish. An ideal partner for discus.

Name	**Bronze corydoras** *Corydoras aeneus*
Origin	Trinidad, Venezuela
Maximum size	up to 7 cm
General care	Easy to keep. At least two should be kept together.
Water quality	Soft to hard Captive-bred specimens are undemanding subjects Temperature 22 to 28 °C
Sexual differences	Males are slimmer. Dorsal fin more extended.
Useful hints	A peaceable catfish that spends the whole day hoovering up the tank bottom, looking for anything remotely edible. Well-suited to the discus aquarium. Not at all choosy about food. Likes food tablets. Captive-bred fish are quite tough.

Name	**Bandit (arched) corydoras** *Corydoras arcuatus*
Origin	Amazonas region
Maximum size	6 cm
General care	Easy to keep. No real requirements in respect of food or water. Best kept in small shoals.
Water quality	Soft to hard Temperature 22 to 28 °C
Sexual differences	Males somewhat larger with a more pointed tip to the dorsal fin.
Useful hints	A very peaceable armoured catfish. Likes the company of its fellows. Breeding possible. Lays eggs on stones or on glass. Eats any food offered. Searches the bottom assiduously for scraps.

Name	**Black-spotted corydoras** *Corydoras melanistius*
Origin	Guayana, Amazonas region
Maximum size	6 cm
General care	Easily kept in the community tank. Not demanding.
Water quality	Soft to hard Temperature 22 to 28 °C
Sexual differences	Outside of the spawning period indistinguishable. Females are somewhat fuller when ready to spawn.
Useful hints	A peaceable catfish that should be kept in small groups. Care and feeding as for the previously-described species of Corydoras.

Name	**Bristle-nosed catfish.** *Ancistrus dolichopterus*
Origin	Amazonas region
Maximum size	10 to 14 cm
General care	Easy to keep. Captive-bred specimens are very adaptable.
Water quality	Soft to hard Temperature 22 to 28 °C
Sexual differences	Males grow to a considerably-larger size and have antler-like growths on their head. The photograph shows a male juvenile.
Useful hints	Accommodating and easily-kept catfish that can be recommended to any discus fan. They like to hide in caves and spawn there too. The male guards the orange-coloured eggs. If at all possible, keep as a pair.

Name	**Plecostomus** *Hypostomus punctatus*
Origin	Southern Brazil
Maximum size	Up to 30 cm but in the aquarium only 20 cm
General care	An easily-kept, nocturnal fish
Water quality	Medium hard to hard Temperature 20 to 28 °C
Sexual differences	Not known
Useful hints	A peaceful, if rather strange-looking, catfish that will help keep the glass of the aquarium clean. Cleans up all kinds of scraps. Discus breeders commonly include this species in their raising tanks so that any food particles will be dealt with effectively. Needs a supply of hiding places. Only put into larger discus aquaria.

PROPER DISCUS CARE

It is often claimed that discus are something of a problem fish. In reality they are anything but problematical and they will put up with a good deal of maltreatment. In fact, they are pretty tough customers. Tetras, dwarf cichlids, many barbs and other small fish species are much more sensitive and susceptible than discus. It is not unusual for very ill specimens to survive for weeks and even months in an aquarium.

They will stop eating, lose weight and just hang on, waiting for their keeper to come up with the appropriate remedy. So here are some basic rules for their proper care which every discus fan should be aware of.

The first essential is probably the need for regular water changes. Under no circumstances should this be neglected. By "regular" what is meant in a planted aquarium, is a weekly water change of about ten

HECKEL discus and wild-caught green discus make suitable companions in a planted aquarium. It is of prime importance, however, that they undergo proper period of quarantine to eliminate the risk of disease.

per cent of the aquarium content. Of course, more is permissible if convenient. In the event that the water can only be changed every second week, at least twenty per cent should be replaced. When carrying out the water change, any solid contaminants should be siphoned off from the bottom. Even this weekly change may be insufficient if the discus are being fed on a

A captive-bred specimen from brown and red parents. This six-month-old fish has a high level of red markings.

high-protein food like ox heart, for instance. With this kind of food you often find that many small particles are left lying on the bed and can quickly bring about a deterioration in the water quality. One way

of overcoming this problem is to put in some bottom-feeding fish like catfish, for instance, which will scoop up such bits. In the absence of such cleaners, these residues have to be siphoned off daily. Obviously, the same thing applies to any mosquito larvae that are uneaten, otherwise the water quality can descend to unacceptable levels. This danger is considerably lessened by using special Discus Food. The effects on fish of food residues in the aquarium is often underestimated. As many of the foods used contain high protein ingredients, these will often quickly turn into toxic substances.

Another factor that can have a detrimental effect on water quality is that certain types of roots may give off harmful substances. Any wood used in aquaria should first be checked to verify its suitability. If water becomes contaminated it should be filtered for a few days over active charcoal.

Discus are often kept in conditions that are too cold. As already explained, they should never be kept at temperatures below 27°. Opinions about the minimum and optimum temperature sometimes vary but experience has shown that discus will thrive above 27°. The epitome of successful discus-keeping is always based on a well-planted, well-maintained tank.

Another prerequisite for success is healthy stock and you would clearly be wise to seek out the best possible fish once you have gone to the trouble of setting up a decent aquarium. Some people are inclined to be slapdash here and look on the quarantine aquarium as something of a bother. Out of these initial mistakes problems arise and the consequences are practically

A nicely suited pair of turquoise discus. The male with its more massive bull-like appearance is on the right. The female also has an amazingly extended dorsal fin with pronounced red colouring.

preprogrammed. For this reason the quarantine aquarium is reckoned to be of utmost importance. It is simpler to treat any sick fish in the confines of a quarantine tank and, at the same time, existing fish in the aquarium will be protected from contact with diseases. The quarantine period should be for at least 14 days. If you manage to ensure that you only introduce fish in tip-top condition into your established aquarium, there should be no major outbreaks of disease. The discus fan must always operate on the basis that any newly-acquired fish, including the discus, is a potential disease carrier. This statement not only applies to wild-caught specimens but also captive-bred fish. After all, water contains many bacteria. Indeed it has to, because there are so many biochemical processes going on in the water that are vital for maintaining its balance. If the aquarium is well planted and the plants are thriving, then it is safe to assume that the aquarium is a healthy environment. The owner of an aquarium that is functioning well should intervene or interfere as little as possible: if it works, don't fix it. Discus are much less susceptible to disease in a well-planted aquarium.

The pH value plays a major part in ensuring proper aquarium conditions. It should be regularly monitored. As long as it is somewhere in the range between 5.5 and 6.5 it should be ideal. With CO_2 additions, the pH value can be in the slightly acidic area if there is no or only a low carbonate hardness. This suits discus. In acidic water, for instance around pH 5.0, bacteria multiply less rapidly and diseases are kept in check.

As soon as the pH value starts to climb above the neutral level of 7.0 you should take action to lower it again. This can be achieved, for example, by the use of peat filtering. However, in the long term, it is only possible to lower the pH by bringing down the carbonate hardness to $1-3°$ dH and by simultaneously giving additional doses of CO_2 at the appropriate concentrations.

THE RIGHT FOOD

In an old book on the subject of feeding aquarium fish I have seen the opinion expressed that the "disc-shaped cichlid" — Symphysodon discus — eats water fleas, Cyclops, white, red and black mosquito larvae and enchytrae. The chapter ends with the remark: "Will not eat dried food. Discus are difficult to tempt with frozen food."

Nowadays it must be said that the opposite is true.

Good flaked or other ready-made foods now represent the main source of food for our captive discus fish. Without the excellent range of artificially-made foods the discus would be even more of a problem fish. It is these foods that enable us to leave our fish in the hands of friends and relatives during holiday absences. And during the working day we can feel safe in the knowledge that any member of the family can be entrusted to administer the right food in the proper amounts. When young discus are still growing they require several portions of food at well-spaced intervals over the course of a day. The first good feed can take place in the morning with between two and five further feeds being given during the morning and afternoon, depending on the size of the fish. Late in the afternoon, having returned home from work, the discus keeper can take over the job and give any special diet that may be required.

Special food for discus fish

After extensive research, Tetra have produced a special purpose-made discus food that has been widely used and with great success by Japanese and German discus fans. Its composition is specifically geared to suit the needs of this species. This food is sold under the name of Tetra Bits in the USA and Tetra Prima in the UK. By happy coincidence it seems that all other companion fish in a discus aquarium take to this food very readily.

It is a fact that discus do present difficulties whenever you try to switch them to a new food. But this problem exists even with live food. Discus that are accustomed to eating frozen red mosquito larvae will very probably reject live white mosquito larvae to begin with. Any changeover needs to be carefully controlled by the aquarist. The new food may have to be offered to the fish on numerous occasions. Any uneaten food should be quickly siphoned off. It may be some days before the first of the discus start to take the new food. However once one or two have started to eat it, it will not be long before all of them begin to take an interest. This is also the case with Tetra's special Discus Food. It should be noted though that smaller discus can be "weaned" on to a new diet much more easily. The fully-grown fish are much fussier. But with patience even wild-caught specimens will adapt to a replacement food with time.

As improbable as it may seem, fish select their own food items. Fish have very good olfactory organs so that the smell of their food is a decisive factor. They can even identify the smallest molecules by smell.

The appearance and colour of the food also play a significant part for discus. Since they also consume hard-shelled food like small crustaceans in the wild, their food should contain items of a more solid consistency. Discus take their food both from the surface and from the middle-water zones. In the aquarium they may also take food that has fallen to the bottom, blowing into the bed material or at any food lying on the bottom to send it swirling upwards. Any items that are found in this way are immediately swallowed. When their food is altered, discus will often repeatedly spit out any hard food, only to swallow it again immediately. Older discus are slow eaters.

These adolescent discus feed greedily on the Tetra Bits Discus Food which contains all the essential ingredients for healthy growth. These youngsters are the "red turquoise" type.

This characteristic should be borne in mind if you are thinking of putting in other species of fish. As most fish, including discus, are inclined to bolt their food, this is transferred straight to the anterior digestive chamber, unchewed and intact. This means, for instance, that mosquito larvae arrive in the digestive tract still live and kicking. This habit of bolting means that harder, solid food, like Tetra Bits, is wholly acceptable.

Discus belong in the omnivorous group of feeders, ie they will eat almost anything, animal or vegetable. Again, within this group it is described as "polyphagous" which is to say that it will accept various

Even fully-grown discus, like this brilliant turquoise male, will easily get used to artificial food.

kinds of food. On the one hand it will take meat-based items ranging from mosquito larvae and shrimps to ox heart. On the other hand, it is quite happy to eat vegetable matter in the form of algae or spinach.

This fact should be taken into consideration when making up its dietary regime.

By its very nature, live food contains an element of vegetable matter that the discus can re-use, "recycle" almost. The same thing applies if you feed them with shrimps. The question of how you supply young discus with vegetable matter when they are being given predominantly Artemia nauplii is another matter. These tiny hatched shrimps must be fed on vegetable matter just before they are fed on to the little discus. A suitable means of doing this is to give them TetraPhyll or a liquid feed.

Discus breeders like to feed their fish on finely-ground ox heart from which the sinews have been removed. Ox heart is by no means suitable as a complete diet; if the fish were given such a monotonous diet they would soon develop symptoms of deficiency. Ox heart can be given if it is enriched with additives. But the high protein content of this food leads to rapid decomposition in warm water so that any scraps must be syphoned off quickly.

Live food requires prior treatment. Most types of live food are also available to amateur fishkeepers as deep frozen packs. This frozen food must be fresh and uncontaminated. Red mosquito larvae in particular, which are a favourite food, can contain harmful substances because, after all, these larvae live and breed around areas of stagnant, not to mention sewage-contaminated, waters. The freezing process does not entirely kill off the pathogens. In this respect, perhaps a better alternative would be freeze-dried food, though this is not always liked by some larger discus. So living or frozen red mosquito larvae should be swilled well in water before they are fed

Tetra Bits Discus Food is especially advantageous in the living room aquarium. Any pieces remain easily visible because they do not break up or cloud the water.

to eat them avidly as adults. Anyone who does not find the job of raising Enchytrae too bothersome will find that these little white worms promote copious spawning in discus females. Another very good form of food are food tablets with a high proportion of freeze-dried live food. Tetra Tips are particular favourites with discus.

One vital factor that cannot be stressed too often is that any uneaten food should be quickly removed from the aquarium.

to aquarium fish. This can be carried out effectively by putting them in a piece of fine nylon stocking and hanging them under running water.

Tubifex worms come from the filthiest of ponds and should therefore not be considered as discus food. A good source of food, though one that is frequently not accepted all that quickly, is black mosquito larvae. If the discus become accustomed to these from an early age, they will continue

SETTING UP A BREEDING TANK

Keeping c ... ough peace and quiet
hobby in ... settle down comfort-
ther and ... raising their young.
This is s ... ng the position you
experien ... e consideration to the
it! ... the surroundings. It is

A dis ... e sides of the breeding
essentia ... aper to ensure the fish
dament ... The tanks should be lit
or even ... d the pair then proceed
Obvion ... ntle night time lighting
accoun ... d.
is poss ... able form of heating for
densel ... s a heating mat placed
cesses ... bottom pane although a
In ad ... m heater will also do. The
ably k ... es must be fitted with
So ... tic controls because a tem-
need ... C is required for breeding
fessio ... temperature of the water is
dispu ... or in ensuring the eggs
aquar ... ature properly.
to me ... nt item of equipment for
overs: ... us breeding is a good, effi-
bonding ... h not too powerful an action.
parents. ... ith a capacity of about 150
with a ... taining only two fish as occu-
quate. 1 ... require much filtering, a filtra-
125—1! ... f appropriate proportions will
not be ... -driven sponge filters have
height ... lent for the job. The Tetra Bril-
to 80 ... ystem has tremendous advant-
lower ... little discus fish or the larvae
becau ... nown to get sucked into the fil-
rium trigger a flight reaction ... rish there. It has even been

Cleaned water,
enriched with air.

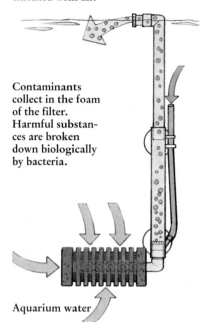

Contaminants
collect in the foam
of the filter.
Harmful substan-
ces are broken
down biologically
by bacteria.

Aquarium water

known for whole broods to vanish into
some filter systems. The foam cartridges
cannot suck in any youngsters. The only
precaution you need take is to position
them so that the young fish cannot swim
between the glass pane and the sponge and
become lodged there. So ensure that there
is free swimming room around the whole
of the sponge.

These effective but simple filters are
operated by air pumps. It is quite possible
to set up several breeding tanks next to one
another and to run them off the same air
pump.

If the breeding tanks are operated with
other kinds of filters that take in water,
then the inlet tube must be sealed off in

such a way that no little fish are dragged in
to the system.

An upturned clay pot will serve as a
spawning place. The prospective breeding
pair will quickly recognise that it constitutes an ideal spawning ground and you

A typical, heavy spawning cone for discus. This
hand-thrown version has two spawning beds and a
dish for the larvae to prevent them from dispersing
too quickly.

can be fairly certain that the female will
choose this place to lay her eggs. If you fol-
low the guidelines outlined in the next
chapter you can be confident that your fish
will produce and raise young.

THE ART OF BREEDING DISCUS

Selecting the right breeding stock

The basis of any attempts to breed discus must be the matter of selecting the right breeding stock at the outset. It is indeed no easy matter to obtain a good pair. It is very rarely that you find a well-matched genuine pair on sale through the trade. What breeder would willingly part with such a prize? Discus fish that are going to be capable of bringing up a brood successfully will need to get on really well. If they are involved in constant disputes it will inevitably end in them eating their eggs or young. Many a breeding attempt comes to naught. Discus form a genuine pair bond, as is often the case with the larger cichlids. This pairing can last for life so this is a further reason for ensuring that any fish you put together are truly suited to each other. As the discus larvae live off the nutrients in the mucous secretions of their parents, the only long-term recipe for breeding success is healthy, well-matched parents.

So just how does one set about acquiring good potential breeders? Since good stock is seldom obtainable through retail outlets, the breeder has to introduce his intended pair to each other. This is not without its problems either, because the sexual differences in discus are so slight and males and females are so difficult to recognise that there is more than a measure of luck involved in selecting the right individ-

uals. The simplest approach is to keep a small shoal of them together until it becomes apparent that a couple of them have paired off naturally.

The different species of discus can also be crossed so that it is possible to induce a brown wild-caught fish to mate with a solid turquoise. Whether the results of the attempt will prove satisfactory remains to be seen. The mistake is often made of keeping every pair that does breed and allowing them to continue to breed — without using a measure of selective judgement. This means that you will go on repeating a mish mash of colours that are not really acceptable. The colour of the parent fish is an an important criterion when selecting breeding material. Brown discus can be crossed with other brown discus. Obviously what you will look for here is the colour intensity, the round shape or indeed the faults in the striping of the parents. By adhering to these selection criteria you will certainly manage to produce well-coloured, strong, round brown discus fish.

However, cross-breeding of captive-bred variants can lead to some particularly bad results where feeble-coloured specimens can inevitably produce throwbacks. Deliberate, targeted cross-breeding can, however, bring about wanted changes and fix desirable characteristics. In a specific instance where one has an inbred stock of captive-bred fish, it can be very useful to cross-breed with wild-caught specimens.

The form, colour, fin conformation and eye colour are all clues that this magnificent brilliant turquoise male is a captive-bred specimen. If you could manage to find a similar female, what an ideal pair they would make.

If, for instance, several generations of turquoise discus have been bred in captivity and certain weaknesses in their conformation start to crop up, they can be improved by cross-breeding with individual selected specimens of green wild-caught fish. By such cross-breeding an increasing number of the wild type colour will occur in the offspring. If these colours are not wanted, a very careful rejection process has to be adhered to in subsequent breeding attempts.

If the breeder places great store in having red eyes in his fish, then obviously he must not use any specimens with yellow eyes for breeding purposes. Even so, evidence of ancestors with yellow eyes is still likely to show through in certain cases where red-eyed parents were used.

It is very difficult to differentiate between the sexes in discus. There are no absolutely reliable sexual characteristics in these fish and even very experienced breeders are liable to make mistakes when sexing their stock. There are just a few little clues but, as already stated, these are somewhat unreliable. The safest way is to observe closely the development of a crop of young discus that subsequently grow up together. In such a specific group the females are almost always somewhat smaller and more weakly-coloured. In such close comparison, the males will probably have a more pronounced elongation of the fin tips. In instances where the dorsal and ventral fins are more rounded, this indicates a female. The pelvic fins in the males are usually more elongated and, seen from the front, are closer together. Discus males often show signs of the typical, bull-like head parts. The only certain way of distinguishing the sexes is at spawning time. The male then displays a pointed spermiduct which protrudes out of the body by about two to three millimetres. The female ovipositor is broader and round, running to about three to four millimetres in length.

If several fully-grown discus are kept together in an aquarium for a length of time, a pair will find each other eventually. They will detach themselves from the rest of the group, occupy a particular territory and lay eggs there. Before spawning, discus develop a typical breeding attire. Some days before spawning takes place the outer rims of the fins take on a dark colour. In some fish the edges may be so dark as to appear black. Of the nine body stripes, the last four to five stand out quite markedly. The tip of the head and tail can appear quite light, though these colour variants vary in intensity. All these features indicate that the fish are ready to breed.

Preparing the breeding tank

Details have already been given about the setting up of the breeding tank. If several aquaria are standing next to one another, it is probably an advantage if the individual pairs can see each other. This "sighting of the enemy" often inhibits the pair from eating their own eggs because the pair in the adjacent tank represents a threat from which the eggs have to be protected. Once the larvae are free-swimming they can be shielded from the gaze of their neighbours by a piece of cardboard to give the pair some peace and quiet to get on with the task of bringing up their young. This task is usually handled initially on a job-share basis with the one fish looking after the clutch of eggs and the other taking care of the larvae that have already hatched. But when it subsequently comes down to just the one job of raising the young, both

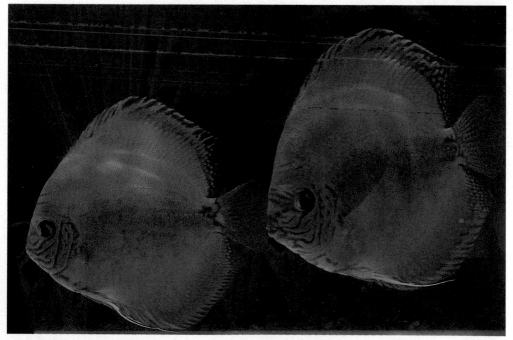

A pair of discus of the "solid blue" type. The female on the left is somewhat smaller. Both fish are exquisitely coloured, though it could be said the amber-coloured eyes are a major shortcoming.

parents take on the role of food supplier. The colour of the bed of the breeding tank should always be kept dark. Black, dark-brown or dark-blue have proved successful shades.

A group of *Symphysodon aequifasciatus axelrodi*, the brown discus.

Name
(Please Print) _____
(Last Name)   (First Name)   (Middle Initial)

Capitol Aquarium

JUL 22 1995

Address _____

City _____ State _____ Zip Code _____

Telephone _____

Drivers Lic. _____

Water preparation

Unlike those discus fans who merely want to enjoy the pleasure of discus-keeping as an end in itself, discus breeders have to become something of an expert in water chemistry. The magic word is water preparation. Discus originate from waters with a very low electrical conductivity. This low level of conductivity in the water is also an important prerequisite for breeding success in captivity.

Every type of water contains salts in solution. These salt ions conduct electricity in the water which is one reason why electricity is so dangerous in the marine aquarium.

The higher the concentration of ions is in a particular body of water, the higher its electrical conductivity will be. The salt concentration in a given water also allows

The male at the rear is standing guard over the eggs. The root that is dangling down from above is that of a Philodendron standing on the aquarium.

you to make certain inferences about its hardness. The conductivity is measured in microsiemens (abbreviation μS). As a general rule of thumb you can work on the basis that 30 μS correspond approximately to one degree of German water hardness (1° dH). In the home waters of discus no carbonate hardness can be measured and the conductivity usually lies around 10 μS, which is to say infinitessimally low despite the fact that there are many sediments, humic acids and trace elements in the water. Through this accumulation the soft, acidic water is also rendered stable. In the aquarium, water with a carbonate hardness of 1° dH and a conductivity of 30 μS will have a very unstable reaction and the pH will drop rapidly. The water ceases to be controllable. This is also the reason why discus breeders like to operate with a somewhat harder water and a conductance level of between 100 and 200 μS. This is without doubt feasible, especially as this water presents fewer problems overall. In any event, water used for breeding should have a conductance of under 200 μS in order to ensure the optimum development of the eggs.

If an intending discus breeder lives in an area where only hard water comes out of the tap, this does not necessarily mean that his dreams are automatically over. All he has to do is to work on what is available to produce something acceptable.

This process of water preparation is carried out through the use of ion exchange resins. These loaded ion exchange resins undertake the task of extracting or exchanging unwanted ions. This may sound rather more difficult than is in fact the case. Indeed, your dealer will probably

A captive-bred male that is rather hard to categorize. It is possible that a royal-blue wild-caught specimen could have been crossed with a green discus or even a turquoise discus. The fantastically beautiful, round, bull-like body form balances out the rather flat turquoise colour. Paired with a brilliant turquoise female, this discus would undoubtedly make a fine founding father of a long line of lovely progeny. The immaculate red eye and the delicate head markings also commend this fish.

have a number of different systems in various sizes. When buying such a system you should always seek specialist advice. For those fishkeepers who would initially like to breed discus in a normal aquarium it is useful to know that an effective softening system at the smaller end of the range is the Tetra AquaTop unit. Here the water is softened by hanging a bag in the water. Where the volume of water is greater and in large-scale breeding tanks it is worthwhile installing a larger exchanger.

If the tap water contains too much carbonate hardness, ie lime, then this can be removed with the help of cation exchangers. The exchanger resin looks like fine sand. The fine resin pellets have to be regenerated with acids and precise instructions are enclosed with the resins. The total desalination of tap water represents a somewhat more difficult task involving the use of two exchange resins. This dual filter process works very slowly. Plastic columns are filled with the respective resin and the water is then pressed through this. The pH value of the water produced in this way then has to be adjusted to suit the discus. One good way of acidifying the water is to use filter peat. As the completely desalinated water is comparable to distilled water it should be diluted with a certain amount of fresh water so as to bring the conductivity to the desired level. By manipulating the water in this way the discus breeder can "compose" his breeding water to his own recipe. However, a word of caution against major changes in pH is called for. Soft, largely desalinated water is very unstable. Discus can be severely harmed by uncontrolled additions of acid. The pH value of a body of water indicates the relative pro-

portions of bases to acids in the water. The neutral figure is 7.0. At this figure there is an absolute balance of the H^+ ions in the acid range and the OH^- ions in the alkaline range. Depending on which of the two ion concentrations predominates, the water becomes either "acidic" or "alkaline". The pH scale runs from 0.0 to 14.0. For discus fish the ideal pH values lie between 5.5 and 7.0 For breeding purposes the figure should be adjusted to around 6.0. Any changes in pH value should be undertaken slowly, excluding the chance of any sudden shock. If this simple guideline is followed changes are largely harmless to discus.

Another method of producing breeding water is to use a reverse osmosis plant. Over the years, various appliances of this type have become available through the trade. In the reverse osmosis process the salt-bearing starting water is forced through a membrane which is impermeable to the salts, bringing about the desalination of the water. Clearly, the above description is only a simplified outline of the operating principle of the reverse osmosis plant. Here again, the amateur is advised to consult the specialist literature on the subject or to seek advice from a specialist.

Reducing egg mortality

One very important factor in discus breeding is the need to reduce egg mortality resulting from the bacteria present in the water, often in large numbers. To some extent these bacteria are necessary in order to bring stability to the aquarium, though conversely, they can attack and kill off eggs. The bacterial count in an aquarium can be lowered by various means though not every method fits in entirely with the notion of breeding. In principle, the use of chemicals and antibiotics should be ruled out because these can be harmful to the parent fish, their eggs and young alike and they can completely destroy what has hitherto been an intact, balanced aquarium environment. There is also a danger that the nutritive mucous of the discus parents could be destroyed. For instance, if preparations containing malachite green or methylene blue have to be used, these have to be filtered out of the water by means of activated charcoal once the larvae have hatched. Only then can you guarantee good mucous production by the parents. The same can be said of ozonization. If ozone is passed into the water using an ozone reactor, the nitrite concentration will be reduced and the bacteria will indeed be killed off. However, ozone must not be used during the period when the parent fish are producing their skin secretions for the youngsters to feed off. Nor should any medicines be used at the same time as ozone. Moreover, the only reliable way of monitoring the ozonizing process is by some expensive measurement techniques.

Another way of lowering the bacterial count is to use UV-filtration. The aquarium water is passed in front of a source of

If the water values in the breeding aquarium are not right, the eggs may easily be attacked by fungal disease. Excessive osmotic pressure destroys the eggs. The eggs turn white which should not be equated with fungal attack.

UV rays. The UV-C radiation kills off the bacteria effectively thus reducing the overall count. Once again, as with any appliances, the operating instructions should be read thoroughly and strictly followed.

Peat also contains ingredients which have the effect of killing off bacteria, so such additions (ie Tetra Blackwater Extract) are highly recommended. The pH value should be checked frequently through the appropriate measurement techniques.

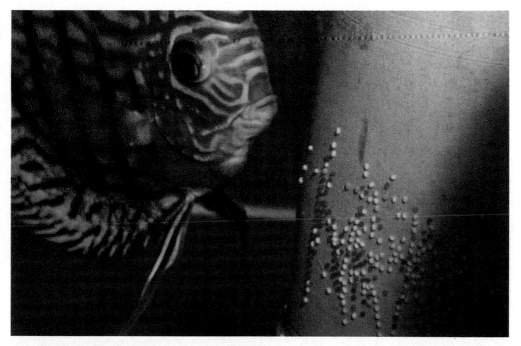

Here the first eggs are beginning to turn dark. The white eggs have succumbed to disease and the dark ones are still viable. They are still capable of producing larvae.

Another very beautiful breeding pair. The male at the front is solid while the female at the rear still has just stripes. Nevertheless, you could still call this pair examples of solid turquoise discus.

Preparations for spawning

Once a discus pair has been found — or rather have found each other — the time will come when they proceed to breed. All the same, it might be quite some time before they get to that stage. And here the discus keeper has to exercise a little patience. The fish will swim up to each other again and again, butting each other gently and without causing any injury.

Actually, it is more a matter of a gentle nudge than a but.

The colour of the fish changes, with the rear half of the body becoming darker. Dark areas become visible in the edges of the fins. The head and the tip of the tail can become a good deal lighter. However, every fish reacts differently. The last four to five vertical stripes are almost always much darker coloured -a sure sign that the fish are ready to spawn.

These fish are preparing to spawn. Here the male is going about his cleaning duties on the spawning cone.

Here the female's efforts to clean the cone are **quite** hectic. The photo overleaf shows both fish sharing the task. Such togetherness can augur successful **breeding**.

The fish take up a position beside one another and begin to twitch, though perhaps the action might be better described as "quake". Real tremors run in waves through the length of the fish. Once these "quake tremors" start, actual spawning cannot be very far off. The next stage is the cleaning of the substrate of the spawning ground. The discus undertake a thorough cleaning of the spawning bed, ie the clay cone, with their mouths. If there are no cones available they will use the heater, the glass pane or the sponge filter or in a fully-fitted aquarium, on bogwood or the large leaves of plants.

This cleaning process may take several hours. During this period the ovipositor of the female will become highly visible. For all that, it may be the next day before the fish spawn. At this point the sex of the fish can be determined with absolute certainty.

119

The female will now decide to take stock of the situation and will glide up to the spawning cone on a trial run. This may be repeated a number of times. The important thing now is to ensure that the male is not distracted. It can happen on occasions that males become so distracted that they omit to fertilize the eggs. If the female starts to lay the eggs from bottom to top, the male has to swim up to the cone repeatedly in order to fertilize the eggs. Experienced, well-suited pairs take things in turns with the female laying one row of eggs after the other. A normal clutch will amount to some 150 to 250, though young females may produce less than 100. However, the number of eggs increases with age. A good result from a spawning would be 200 hatchlings though the average is well below this figure.

The whole spawning procedure takes about an hour. Once it is over, the parents take turns in standing over the eggs, fanning them gently with their fins. Good pairs alternate at regular intervals. The period that the eggs take to develop lasts something like fifty hours and during this time the parent fish can be fed, as is the case later. They should be given small quantities of their favourite food. The initially clear eggs soon show a dark dot and after two days the eyes of the larvae can be made out. The tail of the larvae emerges first and starts to wiggle. This larval stage on the cone lasts a further fifty to sixty hours at which point the first larvae start trying to break away. Actually, they are attached to the spawning substrate by an adhesive thread on their head but soon they manage to break this and free themselves. The parents watch over their brood and collect any escapees in their mouths and spit them back where they belong, for the time being.

This practice of collecting eggs in their mouths gives the impression that the parents are about to eat the larvae. But fear not, they will not do so. Even if it sometimes takes quite a time, eventually they will release the youngsters again. It has proved to be a good idea to leave a subdued night light on near to the aquarium. This gives the parents the opportunity of continuing to watch over their eggs and gives the larvae a better change of finding their way back to their parents.

Once the larvae are free-swimming, it is very important that they have ready access to their parents so that they can begin to feed on the nutrients that exude from their skin.

If this were not the case, the youngsters would start to die of starvation within a few hours. The parents signal to their young with jerking motions and the young begin to feed. They rely on the nutritive mucous of their parents for the first three months of their lives. This skin secretion contains important bacteria that ensure healthy intestinal flora in the young fish. Without this secretion the young fish would be deprived of an important ingredient for their good health in later life. They need to "graze" on this secretion for a least four to six days. No water changes should be carried out during the first week after hatching.

Thereafter you can start feeding the fry Artemia nauplii. At this point the larvae are loath to leave the shelter of their parents' bodies to feed on the Artemia and for this reason the little shrimps should be

These discus are just a few hours old and are already grazing away at the nutritious mucous on their parents' skin. With a magnifying glass it is possible to make out how their little stomachs are filling.

delivered "to the doorstep", so to speak. This can be done using an air pipe or some other narrow tube.

After just a few days the young brave the environment away from their parents' bodies and start chasing after the shrimps in their own right.

The young fish can remain in the company of their parents for up to six weeks, feeding on this skin secretion. Of course, they must be given increasing amounts of high-grade food in which it would be advisable to include several rations of Artemia per day. When the fish have reached

approximately 1 cm in diameter they will gladly start nibbling at Tetra Tips tablets that are stuck to a pane of the tank.

If the parents start showing signs of making preparations for their next spawning attempt, it would be wise to catch the youngsters and remove them to a place of safety where they can be fed on their own. As the young fish are given a very high-grade diet, proper attention to good water care is essential. A partial water-change should be carried out daily.

After four weeks the discus will have grown to the size of a ten pence coin and

Little discus are usually sold at the age of six to eight weeks. They are now the size of an old half crown.

are already very independent, their bond with their parents now on the wane. It is now advisable to transfer them to a larger aquarium because they will grow faster in a more spacious environment. After eight weeks they will reach the size of an old-fashioned half crown and can safely be disposed of, if so desired. After you have your first breeding success, it would make sense to hang on to a certain proportion of the young for a time and even to keep the finest ones indefinitely. When selecting these though, it would be as well to remember that the largest specimens of any given brood are likely to be males. If your only selection criterion is size, then it could easily transpire that you will later be left with virtually no females.

The menace of egg-eating

It is a relatively common occurrence for discus to indulge in the habit of eating their own eggs. In some instances only one of the pair is responsible but it is possible that both will develop a taste for this expensive caviar. The issue constitutes a grave problem for discus breeders.

Just why discus eat their own eggs is still an unresolved mystery from the scientific point of view. Of course, there has been plenty of speculation. Many people claim that the parent fish were too young. But

This is an attempt at protecting a clutch from an egg-eating female. A more satisfactory arrangement is to use a wire-netting device which enables a flow of water to wash around the eggs.

These green discus bred from wild-caught specimens are already ten weeks old. As juveniles, they are not particularly attractive but will soon start to colour up nicely.

how would that account for a case where an experienced breeding pair suddenly start eating their spawn? Because they have been frightened perhaps, or as a protection against feeding rivals. It is so annoying because one would, of course, dearly like to see some kind of outcome from these breeding attempts. The only sure remedy is some kind of radical egg protection measures. For instance, a protective basket can be rigged up out of wire netting with an aperture of up to one centimetre. The wire should have a clearance from the eggs of about one centimetre too. This basket should be positioned over the spawning pot for at least four days. The parents will watch over the eggs and larvae. This protective device should be removed before the young fish are free-swimming. Normally the larvae are no longer in any danger of being eaten. Incidentally, the wire should not be galvanized but rather of fine stainless steel or plastic-coated.

125

A magnificent red turquoise discus from a Czechoslovakian breeding line. This specimen is still very young but has already bred successfully.

Feeding the young fish

The first dietary supplement for discus fish are the small shrimps Artemia salina. These are put into bottles filled with salt water to induce them to hatch. If you have two bot-

tles constantly on the go you will always have an adequate supply of these shrimps in stock. Another good starter food is the Tetra Bits Discus Food. Admittedly, the grains are too big for the larvae, so they need to be crumbled further and scattered

Symphysodon discus HECKEL, the true discus, seen here in an aquarium that really suits it, as shown by its superb colours and general condition. The blue of the head region is particularly striking. HECKEL discus are more difficult to breed than other types and breeders use them for cross-breeding only.

in tiny quantities on the water surface. The larvae will quickly take to them as additional fare.

TetraTips, already mentioned in another section of this book, will also be eaten avidly after two weeks and can easily be boosted with liquid vitamin preparations. Simply apply one drop of the liquid on to the concave part of the tablet. The vitamins will have soaked in after just a couple of minutes and the tablet can then be stuck on to the inside of the aquarium glass.

Tetra Tips are an ideal food for growing discus fish.

An impressive blue wild-caught discus, *S. a. haraldi*. Such fish, with incomplete areas of blue, are sold in the trade as "blue discus". Those with complete blue coverage bear the name "royal-blue".

A splendid captive-bred fish of a very high quality. The brownish-red lines could lead to this fish being described as a red turquoise, though it would also be acceptable to classify this as a brilliant turquoise. It can be seen from this individual that the process of naming captive-bred specimens is often a matter for the beholder. It could be said that every discus is a magnificent fish in its own right.

Providing the larvae with a vitamin supplement is that easy.

A very good, natural food for young growing discus are Cyclops, if they come from waters that are free of fish. These little freshwater crustaceans can be caught or bought deep-frozen. The important thing though, is that they should be of good quality.

At the end of any good feeding session you should be sure to siphon off any residues of food so as to eliminate a potential source of disease.

DISEASE PREVENTION

It is often claimed that the discus is a very disease-prone fish. This statement is not altogether true though. Like any other fish, discus react to wrongful treatment, a deterioration in their water quality, dietary deficiencies and other factors. In its natural habitat the discus could well be classed almost as something of a tough nut and not at all delicate. The primary cause of illness in discus in captivity is unsuitable conditions.

So, an important prerequisite for prevention of disease is good water quality. This is not to say that the discus has got to be kept in extremely soft, acidic water. This kind of acidic water, with a conductivity of around 10 µS as in the Amazon, would be very difficult or impossible to recreate because we cannot lay our hands on the massive quantities of humic acids that go into the natural water. Discus water should have a rather higher conductivity of 100 to 200 µS.

One point that is often neglected is the need for proper quarantine treatment for newly-acquired specimens – and in this respect no distinction should be made between wild-caught or captive-bred fish. All fish should undergo a quarantine period. Unfortunately, many people are apt to interpret this term very loosely with the result that problems can quickly arise. A proven quarantine regime for discus could run along the following lines: the newly-acquired fish are first put into a quarantine

tank the size and type of which will be determined by the financial and phsyical means of the owner and the number of fish being treated. The aquarium is operated with a simple filtration system, based on a cotton wool or foam filtering medium. Filtering charcoal or resins should not be used as filtration media – nor should peat. Where there is a large number of fish to be dealt with, the water is given supplementary aeration via an air stone. The water temperature in a discus aquarium should be 26–27 °C. Higher temperatures prove uncomfortable for the fish, when medicines are being used at the same time.

For general disinfection purposes and to get rid of any skin parasites and trematodes, the use of Contra-Spot is recommended initially, at a rate of 5 ml per 10 litres of aquarium water. After three days this medicine is filtered out over filter charcoal. Subsequently, a third of the water should be changed. The next step of the quarantine procedure is to treat the water with Hexa-ex, a proven remedy for "hole in the head" disease. One tablet should be used for every 50 litres of water. Obviously, the only permissible filter medium is once again foam or cotton wool. After four days up to one third of the water can be changed.

To be on the safe side, the Hexa-ex treatment should be repeated at full strength after about 10 to 14 days. After a further four days the fish that have been treated may be transferred to the community tank. In the course of this quarantine treatment — which may last for some three weeks in all — it is easy to keep an eye on the discus.

Symptoms of disease are easy to recognize. Clearly, the discus will have to be fed during the quarantine and the point that needs to be emphasised yet again is that any scraps of food must be siphoned off. If this involves any great loss of water, remember to top up the doses of medicines as recommended by the maker.

There are many discus that are already in a damaged state when they reach their destination in the home aquarium. Even small discus may be quite ill. Poor water conditions are often an important contributory factor here. Where there are known problems with aggressive tap water it is important that the amateur should address the matter beforehand with the appropriate prior treatment. An initial filtration over activated charcoal and subsequently over filter peat, together with the addition of a water-conditioning treatment, such as Tetra AquaSafe, can provide the solution. Poor water conditions frequently cause damage to the mucous membranes. However, skin and fin damage in discus fish very often heals quite quickly of its own accord but a prerequisite for this healing process is that the biological status of the aquarium water must be at its optimum. It is almost normal for the fins of imported discus to be frayed. This is no reason for not buying a potentially fine specimen.

A common affliction of discus is for them to suffer from "jamming" of one of their gill covers or a quickening of their res-piratory rate. Discus fans would be inclined to diagnose this as a case of gill worms. The first reaction of wanting to resort to strong medicines is actually misguided and not advisable. It actually makes more sense to check over the aquarium parameters, the water and filter. The latter is often overloaded. It might well be that the large amounts of food offered to the fish have produced such a level of contamination of the water that this now represents a prolific breeding ground for "bacteria" and a consequent infection has occurred. A cleaning of the filter, a partial water change and filtering over charcoal for a week will often provide a remedy. Skin worms (Gyrodactylus) may well be present in cases where the discus may suddenly shoot across the aquarium, rub against items of aquarium decor and start to act very timidly. Skin and gill worms (Dactylogyrus) can be identified by examination under the microscope. Medicines to counteract gill worms often do not have the desired effect. In the discus literature one comes across more and more new medicines, usually from the sphere of human medicine. The use of such preparations — which are often not without their complications — ought to remain the preserve of specialists. The bibliography provides the reader with a list of books for further reading on this subject.

Specialist shops also stock treatments for external parasites. As basic remedies GeneralTonic and ContraSpot are recommended and for more stubborn outbreaks of skin and gill worms, Gyrotox® should be used. However, this preparation should only be applied in hardish water with at least 10°d of carbonate hardness and a pH of over 7.0. For this reason the aquarium

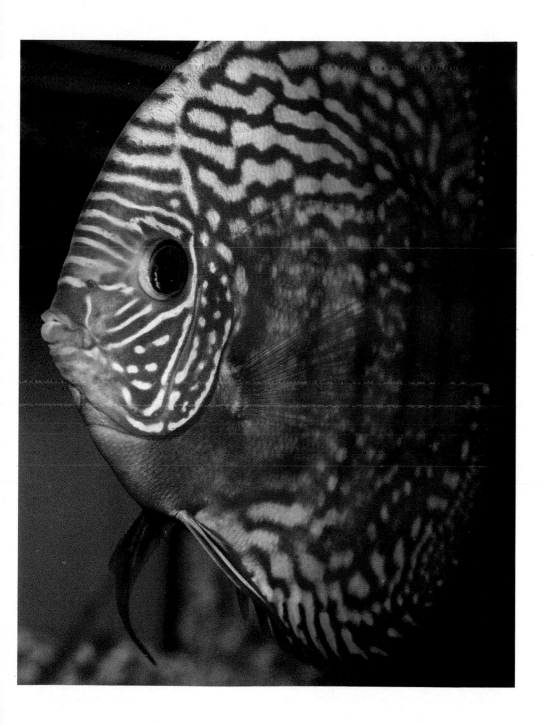

water in which the discus are kept should be hardened. This can be done by using sodium hydrogencarbonate (Na HCO$_3$), available through dispensing chemists (dosage: 30 mg/l 1°dKH). A dessertspoonful of this mixture is dissolved in a glass of water and gradually added to the aquarium water, bringing about a gradual increase in the carbonate hardness and the pH level. Both figures should be monitored by measuring. If the discus are being kept in the water at the time, then the addition of the above solution should be carried out slowly over the course of a whole day. Once the water has been brought up to the prescribed hardness levels, treatment with Gyrotox® may commence.

Clearly, it is not going to be possible to breed discus successfully in such hard water. Breeding grade water can be recreated by partial water changes once treatment has been completed.

To ensure that the treatment has been successful Gyrotox® should be used for a second time. Ten to twelve days after the initial dose of this medicine, a third of the aquarium water should be changed and the same dose as before should be added. NB Check the water values first. After a further 48 hours the medicine can be taken out of the water by filtering over activated charcoal and a partial water change.

The dreaded "hole in the head" disease is the most commonly feared ailment of discus although it does not occur all that often. These holes on the head of the fish are usually triggered by some kind of deficiency or bacterial infections. True "hole in the head" manifests itself through the appearance of a white substance in the head region. Little "whitehead"-like plugs about

1 mm thick and 2 to 3 mm long are exuded. These then drop off, leaving a hole that does not close again. In some cases these holes are very numerous. The first signs of the illness are a general darkening of the fish, a refusal of food and wasting of the body. This is usually accompanied by gelatinous, white faeces, with the stools being trailed around by the fish over long periods. Fresh stools can easily be examined under the microscope for parasites.

As soon as the first signs of hole in the head occur the fish should be treated with Hexa-ex®, repeating the treatment twice thereafter.

The first indications that recovery is on hand is when the fish start eating again. At this point it would be wise to supplement their diet with extra vitamins, the ideal way of doing this being to add a liquid vitamin preparation to their normal food. New DiscusFood can be boosted in this way too. Once the liquid vitamins have been absorbed the food should be given in small portions. By giving such small portions you can guarantee that the fish will have a quick, effective boost to their vitamin intake before the absorbed vitamins get further dissolved in the mass of aquarium water.

The provision of added vitamins via their normal food is of great importance for discus because deficiency symptoms will soon show up where there is a lack of vitamins in the diet. One of the most frequent manifestations is the appearance of holes in the head region. This phenomenon must not be confused with hole-in-the-head disease because the white exudation typical of the latter is absent. The remedy used to counteract this condition in the trade is a combination of vitamins and minerals, such as TetraVital. These can be scattered on to the water or added to the normal food, taking care to read the instructions for use.

First aid measures

It often seems to make sense for sick discus to be removed from their aquarium for treatment. If all the fish in an aquarium have to be treated, it is imperative that you bear in mind that the bacterial flora of an aquarium and its filter can be adversely affected by medicines. Filters can be killed of biologically by their use. The instructions accompanying the medicines must be strictly followed.

Never transfer fish requiring treatment into fresh tap water. Always use water from the aquarium for their treatment.

Disease	Symptoms/Diagnostic Signs
Opacity of mucous membranes Chilodonella Costia Trichodina etc.	Opaque, milky discolouring of skin white spots rubbing, clamped fins
Skin or gill worms	Spreading of gill covers one-sided gill action choking, sticking/jamming of gills increased breathing rate changes in appearance of mucous membranes
Protruding eyes Pop-eyed appearance	Very bulbous appearance of eyes, sometimes on one side only
Flagellates Hexamita Protopalina	Hole in the head, lack of appetite dark colouring abnormal behaviour generally gelatinous, whitish faeces
Fungal infection	Cotton wool-like coating on fish
Ichthyophthirius White spot disease	Initially cloudy discoloration of mucous membranes, then appearance of white spots which multiply rapidly

Possible Treatment Methods	Other Remarks
Treat for 10 minutes in a cooking salt bath at 15g/1 Treat with Exrapid or Tetra ContraIck	In a stubborn outbreak treat with Gyrotox. Monitor water quality carefully!
Treat with Gyrotox strictly in accordance with instructions.	Essential to repeat treatment after 10 days as gill worms may lay eggs.
Immediate partial water change Use Tetra GeneralTonic	Monitor water quality carefully! Keep a close eye on the fish!
Use Hexa-ex as per instructions. Carry out treatment twice.	As soon as fish start eating again, add vitamin supplement to food. Add TetraVital to water
5 ml Tetra FungiStop per 10 l of water	Repeat treatment Pay attention to good water quality and look out for symptoms of disease and lesions.
Treat quickly with Exrapid or TetraContraIck. Repeat as necessary.	Usually brought in by new fish. Keep a close eye on the fish!

Ten golden rules

1. Never overstock the tank. Make sure that the adult discus will be able to form territories. Recognise when enough is enough.

2. Only put in peaceable fish with discus. Do not use large, combative species.

3. Make sure the water quality is right; check the water parameters regularly.

4. Make a weekly partial water change part of your routine. Always siphon off any debris.

5. Do not leave food scraps in the aquarium overnight, because this can generate a lot of undesirable by-products of metabolism. Siphon off any debris in good time.

6. Only introduce any new fish after they have undergone 14 days quarantine and precautionary medical treatment.

7. Provide a good, high quality diet. Supplement food with vitamins.

8. Only use the best quality food. If possible, use food that will generate few waste substances. Live and frozen food is sometimes unacceptable from this standpoint.

9. Keep an eye on filtration. If possible, keep the pH under 7.0 with the help of the filtration material.

10. Keep the plants growing well. Schedule periods of carbon dioxide fertilization. Fish rarely fall ill in aquaria that contain healthily growing plants.

Index

Photographic acknowledgements

Dr. C. Andrews:	57
B. Kahl:	25, 26, 81, 82, 83, 84, 85, 86, 87, 88, 89, 90, 91, 92, 93, 94, 95, 96, 97, 98, 112, 127, 129
C. Kasselmann:	59, 60, 61, 62, 63, 64, 65, 66, 67, 68, 69, 70, 71, 72, 73, 74, 75, 76
H. Linke:	11, 79, 92
Dr. W. Staeck:	12, 24, 38, 122
All other pictures:	B. Degen
Illustrations:	H. J. Eldagsen, R. Tscheschner, W. Wissmann